David Peter Robbins

The Advantages and Surroundings of New Albany

David Peter Robbins

The Advantages and Surroundings of New Albany

ISBN/EAN: 9783337372873

Printed in Europe, USA, Canada, Australia, Japan

Cover: Foto ©ninafisch / pixelio.de

More available books at **www.hansebooks.com**

ITS

ADVANTAGES AND SURROUNDINGS.

HISTORY OF

A PROGRESSIVE MANUFACTURING CITY,

COMPILED UNDER THE AUSPICES OF

THE COMMERCIAL CLUB,

BY

D. P. ROBBINS. M. D.

Author of " Southern Progress," " Health and Happiness,"
Etc., Etc.

INTRODUCTORY.—There are few cities in the United States more favorably located for manufacturing than New Albany. or that have better agricultural and commercial surroundings. Recognizing our natural and acquired advantages the Commercial Club has determined upon a systematic effort to condense a sketch of all our material surroundings into a convenient sized pamphlet for preservation and wide dissemination. On referring to descriptions of the principal manufactories of this place, given in later pages, it will be seen that New Albany is now justly entitled to be considered a prominent manufacturing city, but there is abundance of room for many more industries, and with our superior attractions, the progress in manufacturing developments should rapidly go forward. There are but few cities of New Albany's size in the West, where municipal taxes are as low as here. We have the best of transportation facilities by rail and water; are located on the beautiful Ohio, below the Falls, just at the head of low-water navigation; with two bridges, over which are rapid transit lines, connecting with Louisville. Within forty miles the famous block coal is found, celebrated as a reducing agent in furnaces and, which for the manufacture of Bessemer steel, ranks with the best in the United States. Iron ore, equal to the best Kentucky and Tennessee. is found in this section of Indiana. This is a central point for walnut, oak and hickory timbers. Educational, religious and social advantages are unsurpassed. We have excellent Water Works, and the best of fire protection. The development of the great Southwest within the past twenty years has been phenomenal, and New Albany is the gateway to this flourishing empire. Now that eastern manufacturers are seeking more central and congenial locations for distributing their products over the West and South, by water and rail, why should not New Albany come boldly to the front and assert her superiority? She has direct connection with all the principal trunk lines of railroad and lies directly at the head of low-water navigation, from whence the largest boats may safely go to Cairo, St. Louis, New Orleans and intervening points, at all seasons of the year.

We shall not go into a lengthy preface, but in subsequent pages shall endeavor to bring forth every material feature of advantage to this place; with a view of attracting additional immigrants who seek for health or pleasure, as well as the talents and capital of men of enterprise, desirous of embarking in some legitimate industry. It shall be our aim to avoid lengthy details of unimportant private enterprises or fulsome praise of individuals. The purposes of the Commercial Club and the compiler are, to present in a convenient shape for preservation, as briefly as consistent, a sketch which shall show forth to the world the undoubted superiorities of this city for manufacturing, and demonstrate that our progressive men are ever ready to welcome industrial enterprises. This we have placed in such a form as to insure preservation, while it is inexpensive and will doubtless be mailed far and wide by the promoters of this section.

To the former historians of Indiana and Kentucky, the newspaper fraternity, officials, C. W. Cottom, J. H. Stotsenburg and others of New Albany, the compiler is indebted for many valuable facts which find place in this pamphlet.

PAST HISTORY.—For the purposes of this work we shall give but a brief mention of the remote past. The Ohio Valley is particularly full of interest to the student of American History. Long before the Indians, of whom we have record, roamed the forests of this section, and fished in its rivers and creeks, it is believed to have been inhabited by a superior people—of whom not even a tradition remains—whose only monuments are scattered earthworks, and tumuli here and there, containing bones from a race of giants, pottery, axes, ornaments, &c. Whether these were a distinct people from the Aboriginal Indians or not, we may never know; but it is reasonable to suppose that they were predecessors, or a division of the half-civilized race from whom the Mexican Aztecs descended. Mounds, relics, etc., from these "Mound Builders" were formerly abundant throughout the Ohio and Mississippi valleys, as far north as Lake Superior, and as far east as New York State. If a separate race from the Indians, when and by what agency they were destroyed, will perhaps remain for all time, a mystery as deep as that of the fabled lost island of "Atlantis."

EARLY EXPLORATIONS.—Robert de LaSalle, a bold French adventurer, with his companions and guides, descended the Allegheny and the Ohio rivers in 1669. Some writers say only to the Falls, but LaSalle's own account, speaking of himself in the third person, says: "he followed it to a place where it empties after a long course, into vast marshes, at latitude 37 degrees, after having been increased by another river, very large, which comes from the North; and all these waters discharge themselves, according to all appearances, into the Gulf of Mexico." (Margry, vol. i, p. 330.) This would indicate that LaSalle had followed the Ohio to its mouth, arriving there when the Mississippi was overflown, and the low lands, around Cairo, resembling a vast marsh. Ten years later, LaSalle and others, built a sailing craft of sixty tons burthen, five miles above Niagara Falls, the first boat of white men to sail over the waters of Lake Erie. "The Griffin," as it was called, went as far as Green Bay, Wis., where it loaded with furs, and manned by 15 seamen started with it for the head of Lake Michigan, while LaSalle, Father Hennepin and 20 others went overland to near the site of Chicago, where they waited several weeks for the "Griffin" which was never heard from afterwards. LaSalle and his followers explored the Mississippi, throughout its principal length, taking all this country in the name of France and calling it Louisiana. Early in the eighteenth century, French fur trading posts were established, between Detroit and New Orleans, the route coming up the Maumee to the present site of Fort Wayne, then coming by portage road some fifteen miles to the headquarters of the Wabash; down this stream past Ft. Quiatanon (near Lafayette) and Ft. Vincennes, to the Ohio and Mississippi. Vincennes lays claim to the greatest antiquity in Indiana, dating back to 1702, as the start for their town; but there is no good authority upon which to predicate this belief, as it was a score of years later before Francois Morgan Vinsenne established the fur trading post of that place. A deed bearing date of 1735, signed by Vinsenne and wife, transferred the improvements to his successors, and it subsequently became a military post. The French surrendered this section to the British in 1774, and General Harmar writing from that place, three years later, says: "the town contains nearly four hundred small houses and about nine hundred population."

REVOLUTIONARY WAR.—When the struggles of the Colonies for Independence began, all the lands, northwest of the Ohio, were claimed by Virginia. Kentucky, then a county of Virginia, through George Rogers Clark raised a regiment, with which to fight the British frontier posts. In 1778 he arrived at the Falls and built a fort on Corn island for the protection of his supplies. June 24, he embarked with one hundred and fifty-three men, and by plying the oars, night and day, landed near the mouth of the Tennessee four days later, and marched across southern Illinois to Kaskaskia, where the British post was taken July 4th, and two weeks later the garrison at Vincennes surrendered to the intrepid Clark. By these daring exploits the Indians were made friends of the colonists, and the victories of the Revolution hastened. For the next decade George Rogers Clark was one of the most aggressive men for development, and the Legislature of Virginia, in 1786, in recognition of his valuable services. granted to him and his officers and soldiers 150,-000 acres of land at the Falls, and Clarksville was platted on the Indiana side, now occupied by Howard Park, between New Albany and Jeffersonville. General Clark retired from active life in 1787, and in poverty and sickness lived at Clarksville until 1814, when he was removed to the home of his sister at Locust Grove, near Louisville, where he died in February, 1818. The Assembly of Virginia, in October, 1778, made all northwest of the Ohio river into the county of Illinois, and Col. John Todd was appointed County Lieutenant by Governor Patrick Henry. Arriving at Kaskaskia in May, 1779, he established the first civil government of this section by an election for Judges. Those selected for the Court at Vincennes, were P. Legras, F. Bosseron, Penot, Cardinal, Tulippe, Gamelin, Edeline, Dejinest and Barron. Todd was elected to the Virginia Legislature, from Kentucky the following year, and was killed at the battle of Blue Licks, in 1782. Virginia ceded this section to the General Government in 1784.

THE NORTHWEST TERRITORY.—The area now comprising the great States of Ohio, Indiana, Illinois, Michigan and Wisconsin was, by an act of Congress, created the Northwest Territory in 1787, and aside from the development at Clarksville, the first real American Colony, within this boundary, was platted at Marietta, Ohio, April 7th, 1788, by General Harman, Rufus Putnam, and others. Arthur St. Clair was first Governor, continuing in office until after Ohio was cut off as a special Territory in 1800, all the balance of the area being designated as the Territory of Indiana. A treaty was made by Gov. St. Clair in 1789, with the Indians, but numerous bloody encounters were had with the savages until after Gen. Wayne's decisive victory at Maumee, in 1794. Gen. Harrison, subsequently Governor of Indiana, was an aid-de-camp of Gen. Wayne on that occasion.

INDIANA TERRITORY.—At the census of 1800, this Territory, comprising four times the present area of the State, had 5,641 inhabitants, principally grouped on the rivers and lakes as follows: Mackinaw, 251; other fur traders, on the great lakes, 300; Green Bay, 50; Upper Mississippi, 65; Cahokia, 719; adjoining twp., 286; Kaskaskia, 467; other Illinois points, 886. In Indiana, Clark's Grant had 929; Vincennes, 714; surrounding settlement, 819, and 55 fur traders on the upper Wabash, making about 2,500 inhabitants in the present boundaries of this State, of which 175 were slaves, and 123 free negroes. Those who held slaves under the Virginia and French rule, were permitted to hold these persons in servitude. The question as to whether slavery should come north of the Ohio river or not was long debated, and Jonathan Jennings, was elected to Congress, in 1809, distinctly upon the position of "No Slavery in Indiana." The Third General Assembly, of Indiana, which convened at Vincennes on November 10th, 1810, repealed the "Indenture Law, of 1807," which allowed the importation of negroes, indented in other territories or states and provided for the enforcement of these foreign indentures.

Governor Harrison, through the pressure of public opinion in Indiana, approved the repeal act. So close was the sentiment pro and con, that James Beggs, who was president of the council, gave the casting vote which made the soil of Indiana free from slavery. At this date there were 237 slaves in the area of the present state proper. These continued until death or freedom in other ways, but there was no further introduction of human bondage into Indiana, and the State constitution adopted in 1816, forever precluded its extension.

The act for territorial government was passed May 7, 1800, and a session opened July 4th of that year, at Vincennes; William Henry Harrison having been appointed as Governor; John Gibson, Secretary; Wm. Clark, Henry Vanderburg and John Griffin, Judges. The district of Louisiana, comprising the territory north of latitude 33 degrees, west of the Mississippi river, contained some 10,000 scattered inhabitants at the time of its purchase from the French, in 1803, and the officers of Indiana were authorized by Congress to enact laws for that section; but its people remonstrated, and in 1805, it was made a separate government. Michigan was cut from Indiana in 1804 and Illinois and Wisconsin were taken from it in 1809. The only purely American settlement in the present State of Indiana, at the beginning of the present century, was at Clarksville. Louisville had been established in 1780 and a new fort erected to protect the settlement from Indian forays.

The people of Kentucky petitioned for separation from Virginia in 1783, gained that favor in 1790, and two years later the first daughter, the Commonwealth of Kentucky, was born into the Union.

The embargo laid by Spain upon the navigation of the Mississippi, retarded developments in this section, until it was raised by treaty in 1795, when the river and port at New Orleans were ceded to the United States. In 1802 the treaty was set aside by a transfer of these rights to France, and our Government the next year purchased all of the Louisiana claim from Napoleon, for $15,000,000. The consummation of this transaction opened the Gulf trade to the Union, and the Ohio river at once became an important artery in the World's commerce.

After Indiana was made a territory, there were numerous collisions with the native tribes, during which the treachery and ferocity of Indian character were fully exemplified. The war dances of the Delawares, Miamis and Pottawatomies continued until after the defeat of Tecumseh and his brother "the prophet" at Tippecanoe, on the 7th of November, 1811, when the power of these formidable tribes was effectually broken. The two territorial Governors succeeding Harrison were John Gibson and Thomas Posey, which brings our history down to 1816, at which time Indiana was admitted into the Union. By census taken in 1815 the population was 63,609. Hon. J. H. Stotsenburg owns an original copy of Indiana Territorial laws, published at Frankfort, Ky., in 1802; with revisions of the second and third sessions, printed at Vincennes in 1804. These laws were principally remodeled from the code of Virginia, Pennsylvania and New York, and are signed by Wm. H. Harrison, Governor; Wm. Clarke, Henry Vanderburg and John Griffin, Judges.

INDIANA A STATE.—It would doubtless be of interest to the general reader, if we had space to enter into a more minute description of the early history of southern Indiana, but we shall have to refer the exhaustive enquirer to the published facts regarding those times, having only space in this department to give a brief connection of links. The area of Indiana embraces nearly 34,000 square miles, equal to 21,637,760 acres. Starting at the mouth of the Miami on the east, bounded on the west by the Wabash for 150 miles, throughout the entire length of her southern border, divided from Kentucky, by the majestic Ohio river, crossed in the center by White river, in the northern part, traversed by the Wabash, the Kankakee, and the St. Joseph, with fifty miles of front on Lake Michigan, and with numerous small rivers and creeks in every section of the State, Indiana has an unsurpassed water supply. Her growth in wealth and population, like all the states of the Northwest, has been phenomenal. She now has a population of 2,192,464, while her flourishing cities, her 9,000 miles of iron highway, and her busy manufacturing villas, are proofs of boundless wealth and inexhaustible energy. Indiana is a grand state, having a record for intellectual culture and great writers, second only to Massachusetts, and in many material respects second to none in the Union. In almost everything that goes to make up a live prosperous commonwealth, she is in the front rank. Beneath her fertile soil are found coal, gas, oil, cement and building stone, enough to supply the state for generations. A mild climate, bountiful harvests, and thriving manufactories should tend to make her people contented, prosperous and happy.

The first state officers were Jonathan Jennings, Governor; Robert A. New, Secretary: Wm. H. Lilly, Auditor; Daniel C. Lane, Treasurer; James Scott, John Johnson and Jesse L. Holman, Judges; James Noble and Waller Taylor, U. S. Senators; and Wm. Hendricks, Representative. The State Government opened Nov. 7th, 1816. Upon the first of May, 1813, the Capital had been removed from Vincennes to Corydon, and in 1815, a stone building, 40x40, was erected as a Capitol building. This continued in use until the seat of government was moved to Indianapolis the 10th of January, 1825, since which time the Corydon building has served as a court house for Harrison county. The Capital tavern, where most of the dignitaries lodged, in the earlier history of Indiana as a state, is also of stone, a mile distant from the state house, and is now owned by Joseph J. Terstegge, a prominent citizen of New Albany. In 1834, Michigan claimed that her southern boundary line, should be upon a parallel with the extreme southern point of Lake Michigan, thereby taking South-bend. Elkhart and Toledo in her area. Indiana and Ohio resented the usurpation and the "Toledo war" was inaugurated. Congress to appease the Wolverines, gave to them most of the upper Peninsula and thereby settled the dispute.

FLOYD COUNTY.—This County was named from Davis Floyd, an adherent and chief adviser to Aaron Burr in is notorious Ohio river expedition, later a member of the Territorial Legislature and first Circuit Judge of this section. Floyd county, excepting Ohio, is the smallest county in the State. It was cut from Clark and Harrison in 1819, and contains 92.800 acres, about 145 square miles. It presents a great diversity of flats, hills, valleys and bottom lands. A range of knobs, formerly known as the Silver Hills, crosses the county from North to South, nearly touching the river at the lower end of New Albany, and by their semi-circle to the westward largely protecting the city from storms and cyclones. The county is well watered by a dozen fair sized creeks and many smaller tributaries, which flow into the Ohio river on its southern boundary. Formerly covered with forests of oak ash, hickory and walnut it yet has small tracts of valuable timber. The bottoms are a rich alluvial soil, and raise heavy crops of corn, oats and potatoes, while the hills produce good wheat and other cereals, tobacco, etc., and the up-lands furnish fine crops of grass and hay; grapes, berries and fruits thrive well in all portions of the county, large orchards abounding n both the high and low lands. In fact it is conceded that a principal source of income for this section should be in fruit raising; as grapes, strawberries, apples, pears, peaches, etc., are seldom injured by frost, and grow to perfection when wisely selected and properly cared for.

With the metropolis of Louisville at our very doors a home market is always certain and the excellent transportation facilities afforded by rail and water invites competition.

There are numerous quaries o limestone, freestone, and a superior sandstone for building and other purposes. The breeding of fine stock is now attracting general attention among the farmers, and the conditions are favorable for the production of thoroughbreds. Blue grass indigenous, pure water is abundant, the climate is mild and there is no good reason why experienced stockmen should not make a decided success in Floyd. Improved farms in the interior have never struck speculative prices, ranging from $20 to 7 per acre; bottom lands $75 to $100; while tracts within five miles of New Albany command a much higher figure according to their desirability. In the immediate vicinity of this city, the rugged bluffs are being transformed by artificial labor, into beautiful and picturesque tracts, of which "Silver Hills" plat is among the most prominent and will be mentioned in detail further on. The elevation of these hills above the surrounding country gives a magnificent view, and since, by the Highland Electric Railway, they have become accessible, healthy summer homes and excursion resorts for the people of the "Falls Cities" will now become general.

EARLY SETTLEMENT.—The first permanent settlement in Floyd county was in Franklin twp., in 1804, by Robert LaFollette; Patrick Shields soon afterwards settled in Georgetown, and Germans in various other places. The first settlers within the present limits of New Albany were James Mitchell, the ferryman at the foot of E. 5th street about 1809, and Mr. Trueblood who erected a log grist mill on Falling Run, near the site of the depot of the L., N. A. & C. R. R. Mr. Marsh built a cabin near by, and a Mrs. Roberts kept strangers, the mail carriers from Louisville to Vincennes stopping here and bringing the local mail to the self-imposed first postmistress in this county, before New Albany was founded. Col. John Paul, of Madison, sold fractional sections, 2 and 3, to Joel, Abner and Nathaniel Scribner, in 1812. The cutting of timber for log house development began March 2d, 1813, shortly after which a double log house was erected in this place. New Albany was platted in the fall of 1813, and some lots sold. It was incorporated 1817 by Scribner Brothers, John Eastman and Charles Woodruff. Col. Paul had taken up this land in 1808, believing that it would make a valuable site from its close proximity to the Falls, and because its central plateau was entirely above high water mark, while even the lower bank is only overflown by remarkable floods. The Scribners in addition to this, discovered an excellent mill site and place for a future manufacturing city, and notwithstanding that the price asked by Col. Paul was nearly $10 an acre, an excessive figure for wild lands at that date, they contracted to pay $8,000 for the tract of 826 acres.

Nathaniel, father of the Scribner brothers, served in the Revolutionary war, and died in 1800, leaving a family of 12 children and a widow. Eliphalet Scribner, the eldest of the family, went to the West Indies about 1800, and became rich. After the founding of New Albany, Eliphalet dispatched a cargo of sugar to New Orleans, consigned to his brother Abner, who arrived there in 1814 ahead of the cargo, and receiving the manifest while the vessel was yet in the jetties, he succeeded in selling the boat and its load to General Dent, (later father-in-law to President Grant,) for the sum of $20,000. A portion of this money went to pay Col. Paul, although it was a dead loss to Col. Dent, as the boat sunk before arriving at the wharf.

Nathaniel Scribner died in 1818, after having secured the formation of Floyd county. Joel died in Oct., 1823, and Abner, who had erected a steam saw and gristmill here in 1814-15, another in Ky. some years afterwards, and in Memphis about 1825, died in the latter place of yellow fever, in 1827. Abner Scribner used to say that the world would yet revolve around New Albany, and delighted to expatiate on the great water power for manufacturing developments. The value of a sharp descent in a great river, like the one we have at the Ohio Falls, has ever been prominent in engineering minds, in many places successfully utilized, and on later pages we shall attempt to show how this can be accomplished here through the construction of a canal, turbine water wheels, and the recent inventions which demonstrate the possibility of conducting electrical power to any required distance. See "River, Canal, etc."

COUNTY GOVERNMENT.—Upon the formation of the county, Davis Floyd was made Judge; Isaac Van Buskirk, Associate; Joel Scribner Clerk and Recorder; James Besse, Sheriff and Treasurer; and Isaac Stewart, Assessor. Court opened May 19th, 1819. Charles Paxson, Clement Vance, Jr., and Jacob Piersol were the first Commissioners. The Commissioners met first at the house of Seth Woodruff, and continued to make that their official place for several years. On Feb.

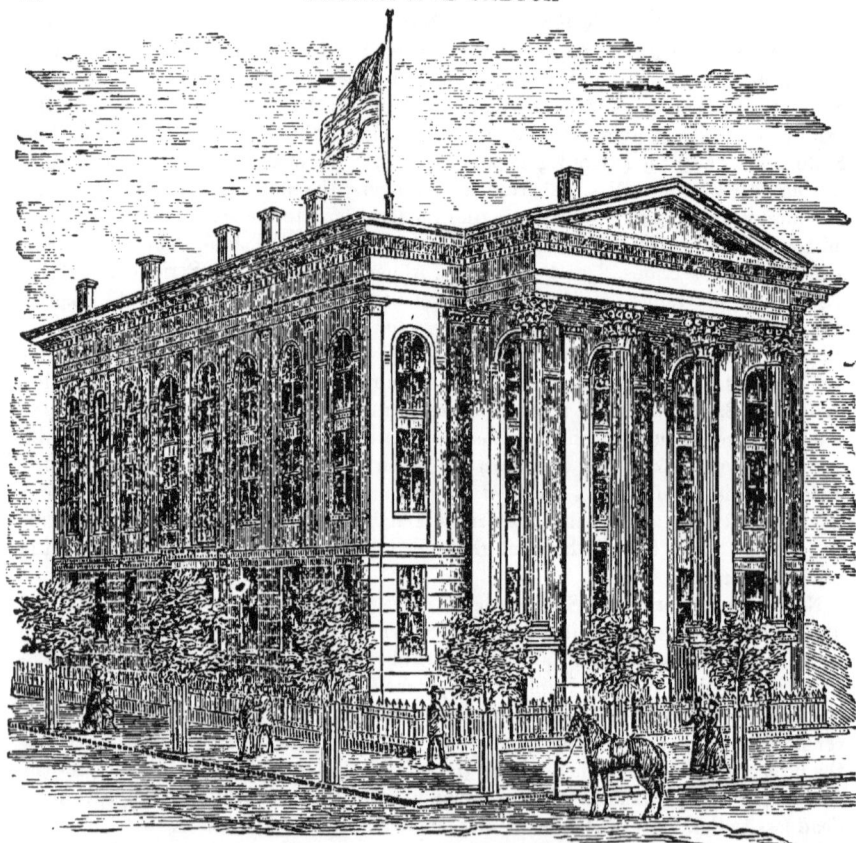

FLOYD COUNTY COURT HOUSE.

10th, 1819, the Commissioners "ordered that the tavern keepers, within the county of Floyd, observe in their taverns the following rates, to-wit: For breakfast $31\frac{1}{4}$ cts; dinner, $37\frac{1}{2}$ cts.; supper, 25 cts.; lodging, per night, $12\frac{1}{2}$ cts.: peach or apple brandy and gin, $18\frac{3}{4}$ cts. per pint; Jamaica spirits, per half pint, $37\frac{1}{2}$ cts,; corn or oats, per gallon, $12\frac{1}{2}$ cts." In 1824, lodging was reduced to $6\frac{1}{4}$ cts.; breakfast and supper, to $18\frac{3}{4}$ cts., and dinner to 25 cts.

On May 3rd, 1819, Seth Woodruff was paid $50 for building a jail, and the total expense, for this first year of Floyd county government was but $208.97. The state and county tax for 1820, was $1,210.40½. On May 24th, of that year, Absolom Littell was fined $6 for refusing to accept the office of Overseer of the poor.

The succession of Commissioners, as the historian has traced them from the records, from year to year, were D. H. Allison, 1820; Josiah Aiken, '22; Mordecai Collins, '23; W. W. Winchester, '24. A new law, at this time, placed the county affairs in the hands of a Board of Justices, who convened Sept. 16th, 1824, with Lathrop Elderkin, president; David M. Hale, president, 1828; Elderkin again in '30; Charles H. Clark, '31. Sept. 5th, 1831, the government returned to Commissioners with Robert

Downey. James Gregg and Gilbert Budd, as the Board. Dan'l Keller, elected 1832; Jacob Anthony, '34; James H. Hills, '35; James T. Duncan, 36; Isaac Stewart '37; John Rice, John Brown, '38; Josiah Lamb, Jacob Summers, '39; James Burger, '41; Augustus Turner, '43; Thomas Piers, '45; Duncan again in '48; Albert Gregg, '48; Green H. Neeld, '49; James P. Tyler, '50; Piers again in '51; Stewart Sandford, '52; Joseph Blunk. '53; Samuel Williams, '54; Charles Duncan, John Jones. '56; Wm. Z. Aydelott, '58; John G. Tompkins, 60 ;Charles Sackett. '61; Moses Harper, '62; W. P. Swift, '63; J. B. Hancock, '64; Hiram Hopper, '66; Neeld again in '67; Anthony Mottweiller, '68; Henry S. Perrette, '69; Ludwig Hurrle, James Tabler, '71; William Cook, '73; J. H. Jones, '74; Peter R. Stoy, '75; Francis Collins, Michael Riley, '77; Albert Bullard, Peter Jacques, '78; Wm. R. Atkins, 80; G. W. McClintick, James Taylor, '82; John Smith, 84; John L. Rafferty, '88; Nicholas Knabel, '89; James Williams, '90; Isaac B. Friend, '91; the three last named being the present efficient Board. Mr. Friend is a manufacturer of this city, under which heading he will have mention; Nicholas Knabel is a prosperous farmer of Edwardsville, Georgetown tp., while James Williams is also in agricultural pursuits, at Greenville, this county.

AUDITORS.—We can find no record of Auditors prior to 1845, the Commissioners or their clerks apparently having officiated in that capacity. Since then the names have been as follows: Augustus Bradley, '46; Dudley D. Byrn, '55; Charles Sackett, '63; Thos. J. Fullenlove, '71; Thomas Hanlon, '75; Andrew B. Weir, '83; and Robert W. Morris, the present incumbent, who was elected in 1886, and reelected in 1890, for a second four years term. Mr. Morris is a native of this city, educated in our home schools, and served for two terms as city Clerk, just prior to his election as Auditor. He is a careful and efficient officer, and has inaugurated several improvements in his department.

SHERIFFS.—In early history the Sheriff was also Treasurer; James Besse having filled the office till 1824, when he was succeeded by P. F. Tuley; Gen. Alex. S. Burnett, prominent in the early history of New Albany, 1827; Benj. S. Tuley, 31; Wm. M. Akin, 35; S. G. Wilson, 39; Jacob Anthony, 41; Thomas B. Walker, 45; Thomas Gwin, 49; Thos. Akers, 52; John A. McIntire, 54; Charles Frederick, 56; John Wilcoxson, 60; Steward Sandford, 62; T. J. Fullenlove, 66; George W. Jones, 70; L. S. Davis, 74; John Hahn, 76; H. K. W. Meyer, 80; Jacob Loesch, 84; and John Thornton. the present Sheriff, who was elected in 88, and reelected in 90. Mr. Thornton is a native of Ireland, and was formerly in the mercantile business at Edwardsville. Edward L. Kelley, an old resident of New Albany, has been Deputy Sheriff during Mr. Thornton's administration, and is thoroughly acquainted with the duties of the office.

COUNTY TREASURERS.—The Sheriffs were *ex-officio* Treasurers until the forties, when it was made a separate office. The first Treasurer whose name we find separate from the Sheriff, was Wm. Speake, 48; Peter Yesley, 52; Wm. A. Tabler, 55; Philip M. Kepley, 56; Charles Duncan, 58; W. L. Smith, 62; Valentine Graf, 66; Samuel W. Waltz, 70; W. F. Frederick 74; Frank S. Devol, 78; Isaac Miller, 80; W. R. Atkins, 84, and L. H. Scott, the present Treasurer, who was elected in 88. Mr. Scott is a native of Lafayette tp., in this county, and was early engaged in school work. He graduated from the Bedford college in 1875, and the Valparaiso Normal school 78; continuing in school work, he was appointed County Superintendent in 81, and again in 85 and 87, serving up to about the time of taking the Treasurer's office. James H. Scott, of the same tp., has been Deputy Treasurer during Mr. Scott's administration.

COUNTY CLERKS.—Joel Scribner was the first Clerk and Recorder, succeeded in 1823 by Harvey Scribner; Franklin Warren in 36; H. W. Smith, 36; I. N. Aiken 47; Salem P. Town, 53; W. W. Tuley, 61; B. F. Welker, 70; J. B. Mitchell, 78; H. R. W. Meyer, 85; and Frederick Sauer the present incumbent, who was elected in 90. Mr. Sauer is a native of this city, educated in the public schools, and has been Deputy in the Clerk's office for fifteen years past, fully understanding its duties. John W. Gaither, a native of New Albany, who graduated from the N. A. Business College in 90. has given entire satisfaction as Deputy under Mr. Sauer.

RECORDERS.—As before mentioned, the County Clerk was also Recorder up to 1833, when Aaron S. Armstrong was chosen; Wm. Hardia, 36; Sam. H. Owen, 44; Geo. H. Harrison, 55; James G. Harrison, 57; Josiah Gwin, 61; John Spelman, 70; F. M. Spelman, 74; Charles Schwartzel, 78; Chas. W. Schindler, the present Recorder, was elected in 86, and reelected 1890. He is a native of this city, a plasterer by trade. Mr. Schindler is a graduate of the Ohio State Normal School at Lebanon, and taught for six years. He is assisted in the duties of Register by his sister Miss Fannie Schindler, formerly a pupil of the New Albany Business College.

COUNTY SURVEYORS.—The Surveyors of Floyd county have been Benj. Gonzales, 48; John Taylor, 53; L. F. Hand, 57; Geo. M. Smith. 64; F. J. Sweeney, 88; and E. B. Coolman, elected 90. Mr. Coolman is a native of Ohio; graduated at the Ravenna academy, and has been in civil engineer work since 1864. He was with the locating corps of the Air Line R. R., in 71, and in 72 had charge of a division. He has since served in government and railroad surveying until coming to New Albany in 1883.

CORONERS.—The Coroners have been Wm. B. Green, 35; John Peyton, sr., 43; Abraham Baxter, 54; John Sinex, 56; Geo. W. Self, 58; Sinex again, 75; E. L. Pennington, 74; Elijah Whitten, 76; J. H. Lemon, 80, and Wm. L. Starr, the present Coroner, noticed in the medical profession.

CIRCUIT JUDGES.—Up to 1890, the Circuit Judges served also for Clark county, and formerly several other counties were in the district. The first Circuit Judge was Davis Floyd, succeeded by John F. Ross, 23; John H. Thompson in 34; Wm. T. Otto, 45; Geo. A Bicknell, 52; John S. Davis, 76. S. K. Wolfe was appointed on the death of Judge Davis, until the election of Charles P. Ferguson in 80; Judge Bicknell took the office again in 1890, but only served two terms of the court, dying suddenly April 11th, 91, when George V. Howk was appointed and served until his death, Jan. 13th, of the present year. Jacob Herter served for five days, when George B. Cardwill was appointed by Gov. Chase. Judge Cardwill was born in Cincinnati, Ohio, 1846. coming to New Albany in boyhood. He read law with John H. Stotsenburg. was admitted to the bar in 1874, and has since been in practice here. Judge Cardwill has been an active member of the Commercial Club from its start and has shown a deep interest in New Albany's upbuilding.

The Associate Judges up to the time of the abolishment of that office were Seth Woodruff, Clement Nance, Patrick Shields, John Conner, William Williams, Wm. Underhill, and Thomas Sinex.

Seth Woodruff served as Probate Judge from the organization of that Court up to 1852, when Joseph A. Moffatt became Judge, and next year it was made a Common Pleas Court, with Nathaniel Moore as Judge. Alex. Anderson succeeded in 56; Geo. V. Howk, 58; D. W. Lafollette, 59; Amos Lovering, 60; P. H. Jewett, 64; Chas. P. Ferguson 72, who continued until the Common Pleas was merged into the Circuit Court.

The Criminal Judges were J. H. Butler, appointed in 68; Cyrus L. Dunham, elected, 68; Thos. L. Smith, 72; who continued until the office was abolished.

TOWNSHIP TRUSTEE.—This is quite an important office, having in its jurisdiction the principal financial and progressive features of the township. The present incumbent for New Albany twp. is David Harbeson, a native of Harrison county, who came to this city in boyhood, and was for many years in the pork packing and livery trade. Henry Harbeson who was educated in the city schools, and at the New Albany Business College, is assistant and deputy.

NEW ALBANY AS A CITY.—This place was incorporated as a city in 1839, and while she has never had *a boom*, her development has been steady and continuous. The recent erection of the cantilever Kentucky and Indiana bridge, making the second rail connection between this place and Louisville, and the building of the Highland Railway last year, are important additions to our advantages and will assist in bringing rapid development. New Albany's city limits have not been extended, like many places of this size, to cover an unwarranted area, but with her suburban developments the population, within a radius of two miles from the court house, is more than 25,000, and as it is flanked on the west and northwest by the beautiful "Silver Hills," which form a picturesque back ground, having most of its buildings above high water mark on an elevated plateau, just at the foot of the Ohio River Falls, it is particularly well located for future developments. To these natural, advantages have been added well paved and well lighted streets, a superb water supply, electric light and rapid transit, making the city and its suburbs especially desirable. The wagon roads into the surrounding country are generally macadamized or graveled, and by reference to subsequent pages it will be seen that this is a railroad centre of no mean importance, with good prospects of continued developments in iron highways.

Eighty years ago New Albany and Floyd county had not been born, and the site of this city was an unbroken wilderness, with Falling Run on the north and the Ohio river on the south. But the soil was rich in the elements which minister to the enjoyment and sustenance of civilized humanity, and the Scribners purchased 826 acres from John Paul, who had located it before. The beautiful woodlands gave way to utilitarian demands, and others, who came later, saw a grand opportunity for developments into a manufacturing city. But the aim of this publication is to give present advantages and prospective statistics and facts, which shall make this pamphlet worthy of preservation for reference by future generations.

The increase in population has never been spasmodic, and during the decade from 70 to 80, a reduction of the city limits, and a combination of adverse circumstances, left us with but little advancement, but with that exception, we have increased 25 per cent in population with each decade, and between 80 and 90 our additions were fully 33 per cent. The increase for two years past has doubtless been in a much greater ratio, and it is fair to assume that the present population of New Albany, with its suburbs. is at least 25,000. At the incorporation in 1839, the population was 4,200; 1850 showed 9,785; 60, 12,000; 70, 15,396; 80, 16,423; while in 1890, the census showed nearly 22,000, exclusive of large suburbs just outside of the city limits, which are properly a part of the regular development. We intend that the pages of this pamphlet shall contain a retrospect of not only the past, but New Albany as it now is, its surroundings its industries, its trade, its social advantages, and plans for future and continued development, and to that end shall endeavor to incorporate statistics or other information worthy of perusal on every page.

CITY GOVERNMENT.—The manner in which a city government is conducted is of vital importance to the growth and business interests of the place. Upon the character and wisdom of its legislation and the faithful execution of municipal laws, much of the prosperity of any city depends. In New Albany's history the fidelity of its officials, and the wise direction of its affairs have been the general rule. Instances of incompetency, dishonesty, or unsavory rings have been very rare indeed.

The first New Albany city officers were P. M. Dorsey, Mayor; Henry Collins, Recorder; John S. Davis, Clerk; Edward Brown, Treasurer; David Wilkinson, Collector and Marshal; Patrick Crowley, James Collins, Israel Crane, Edward Brown, Hezekiah Beeler, Samuel M. Bolin. H. W. Smith, R. Crawford, Absolom Cox, Wm. Underhill, Preston F. Tuley and E. W. Benton, Councilmen.

MAYORS.—The succession of Mayors has been Shepard Whitman, 40; Silas Overturf, 43; James Collins, 44; Wm. Clark 44; Wm. M. Weir, 47; J. R. Franklin, 49; Weir, again, 50; Alex. S. Burnett, 52; Jos. A. Moffatt, 53; J. D. Kelso, 55; Franklin Warren, 56; Burnett, again, 59; D. M. Hooper, 63; W. L. Sanderson, 65; Wm. Hart, 68; Thos. Kunkle, 71; W. B. Richardson, 74; Sol. Malbon, 77; B. C. Kent, 79; J. J. Richards, 83, and Morris McDonald, the present incumbent, who was elected in 89, and relected 1891.

MR. McDONALD was born at Centreville, Ohio, Nov. 10, 1836; came to New Albany in 1843, and was early engaged in the pork packing business, in which he met with excellent success. Later he became a stockholder and general manager of the New Albany Railmill, which business developed largely under his direction. Mayor McDonald operated extensively in grain buying, and has been largely interested in steamboats, real estate, banking and other developments of this place, having gained a wide reputation as a successful business man, and thoroughly enterprising citizen.

CITY CLERKS.—John S. Davis was succeeded by Joseph P. H. Thornton, 42; S. W. Cayce, (1 month), 44; Wm. A. Scribner, 44; Elijah Sabin, 52; William W. Tuley, 56; R. M. Weir, 61; M. I. Huette, 67; Wm. B. Jackson, 77; Robt. W. Morris, 83; Robt. F. Kraft, 87; and Ben. J. Hinkebein, the present clerk, was elected in 1891. Mr. Hinkebein is a native of this city, educated in the public schools of New Albany, and served as a mechanic prior to his advent into this office.

CITY TREASURERS.—Edward Brown was succeeded by Thomas Danforth, 44; Abram Cayce, 50; S. M. Dorsey, 51; Michael Streepey, 55; W. M. Weir, 56; T. J. Elliott, 57; Dorsey, again, 59. Geo. Gresham, 61: S. Malbon, 67; S. M. Weir. 75, and Jacob Best, the present treasurer, was elected in 89, and reelected, 91. Mr. Best was born in this city, Dec. 5, 1855, and educated in our public schools. He learned the cigar maker's trade, and was engaged as proprietor of Manufactory No. 136, for 13 years prior to his election as city treasurer.

CITY MARSHALS.—D. Wilkinson was succeeded by Jacob Anthony, 40; M. C. Foster, 41; Aug. Jocelyn, 44; Robt. Mercer. 44: James Newbanks, 45; Wm. B. Green, 48; Jeremiah Warner. 51; Paul E. Slocum. 53; S. M, Bolin, 54: Newbanks, again, 55; Berry Gwin. 56; Thos. Akers, 58; Thos. Kendall, 71; D. W. Carpenter, 75; Herman Fine, 81; Louis C. Hipple, 85; W. C. Meyers, 89, and reelected 91. Mr. Meyers is a native of New Albany, educated in the public schools, and was engaged as a mechanic in the Rolling Mill prior to his election as city Marshal.

COUNCILMEN.—We have not space to give the long list of Councilmen who have officiated in the past 53 years, it will suffice to say, that they have been men of good judgment and business enterprise. The city has six wards with two Councilman from each, the names at present being as follows: First Ward, Geo. F. Penn and Louis Groh; Second Ward, Frederick Wunderlich and Frank Fougerousse; Third Ward, H. B. Loughmiler and F. B. Zeigelbauer; Fourth Ward, John Heib and John Mathes; Fifth Ward, Wm. Sloemer and David Natius; Sixth Ward, Wm. Perry and Perry Lewis.

CITY ENGINEERS.—H. B. Wilson was chosen city Engineer 1850; L. B. Wilson. 56; John Taylor, 58; Geo. M. Smith, 63; Hart Vance, 77; C. O. Bradford, 79; Smith again, 81; E. B. Coolman, 88, and S. T. Mann elected 1890. Mr. Mann is a native of New York City, and came here in 1870, on the engineering force of the Air Line, having from 80 to 90 served as assistant engineer on the Air Line Ry. W. H. Murphy, a native of New Albany, educated in her public schools, for four years in the fire department, has been assistant city Engineer since 1888.

POLICE FORCE·—The general character of our laboring classes is peaceable. Strikes and riots are seldom known. and a small force of policemen is sufficient to preserve the peace. The patrolmen are Thos. Smithwick, A. L. Sharpe, Dennis Gleason, sr., Charles Winn, Ed. Barrett, Jas. Reasor, Frank Richards, Jacob Fess, sr., Lorenzo Daily, Peter Silz, Philip Strack, Louis Belvois, jr., Wm. Jenks, James W. Dennison, Chas. Tucker and Benj. Murphy.

The Chiefs have been D. B. Star, 70: Joel D. Smith, 71; Wm. A. Carpenter, 73; Benj. Bounds, 75; D. W. Carpenter, 76; Wm. A. Carpenter, again in 78; Thos. E. Spence, 79; Thos. Smithwick. 80; David Balthes, 81; Richard Schindler, 82; S. T. Finney, 83; Louis C. Hipple, 85; (5 months.) Smithwick to fill vacancy. and elected 86; John Marrs, 87; John Stone·ipher, 89; Jos. Featheringill. 90, and Thos. J. Cannon 91. Mr. Cannon is a native of New York; has resided in New Albany from childhood, and has been in the police business for the past 17 years.

FIRE DEPARTMENT.—But few cities of New Albany's size can boast of a better equipped or more efficient fire department than this. The record of disastrous fires, within the city limits, has been very rare, and insurance is written at a reasonable rate. The machinery of the department is in excellent condition, the best of horses are kept, and the equipment throughout is modern in all respects. All the members are paid for their services, and work with military precision. At this writing, (March 92), there are four reels and a hook and ladder; but these are to be reinforced, in the immediate future, by two additional reels, and the necessary men, of which note will be found on a later page, "additions, omissions, etc." There is also a good steam engine kept in reserve, but as we have an average pressure of 75 to 85 lbs., the engine is seldom needed. The Chief Engineer of the department receives $800 per annum, and the men each $1.75 per day.

The Chiefs have been V. A. Pepin, 53; Wm. M. Weir, 54; Chas. Wible, 55; Peleg Fiske, 56; Ed. Q. Naghel, 57; Jasper Blythe, 59; Thos. Akers, 62; John H. Dorst, 63; Stephen Stuckey, 64; Wm. B. Plumer, 65; Wm. Merker, 67; Everett Wattam, 78; Merker again, 80; Joseph A. Adams, 81; Merker again, 83; Charles W. Mathews, 85; and Wm. Merker, for the fourth time in 89, having now served seventeen years in this capacity, which is a sufficient guarantee of his ability. Born in this city March 17th, 1834, and connected with the departments since 49, Mr. Merker does not hesitate to ascend a ladder, or scale a dangerous position, with the same dexterity as younger members of the force.

James Monroe Merker, son of the above, officiates as Secretary and Superintendent of the fire alarm telegraph, and David Beard is Assistant to the Chief, as well as Captain to the hook and ladder. The department has 5,000 feet of first class hose, four substantial brick buildings and is manned as follows:

Reel No. 1—Captain, Harry Hatfield; Pipeman, Benj. Truman; Driver, James Williams. Reel No. 2—Captain, George Dishman jr.; Pipeman, John Plaiss; Driver, Joseph Featheringill. Reel No. 3—Captain, Charles Harbeson, Pipeman, Anthony Neafus; Driver, Archie Wilton. Reel No. 4—Captain, Victor Herbst; Pipeman, Ed. Bonifer; Driver, Roscoe Davis. Hook and Ladder—Captain, David Beard; Laddermen, John Briggs and Taylor Cashman; Driver, Richard Hollis.

The average calls are about one fire every three days, 120 runs having been made in 1891.

CITY LIBRARY—Extensive reading leads to culture and refinement, and with a library aggregating more than 7,000 volumes, and growing at the rate of 1,000 volumes each year, there is no excuse for any citizen of New Albany to be without reading matter to suit his taste. This is absolutely free to every resident of the city, or to those owning property here, and covers history, biography, travels, fiction, poetry, science, essays and general literature, political economy and government, juvenile and reference books. The library has 3,000 regular patrons and is under the management of the school trustees. The library association was organized in July, 1885; through the influence of Judge Cardwill, J. H. Stotsenburg, E. S. Crozier, J. W. Clokey, and others, for four years, remaining at Y. M. C. A. rooms, when it was moved to No. 12, E. Main, its present quarters. Its steady increase will doubtless require the erection of a permanent home for this public benefit in the near future. Jas. H. Ashabranner succeeded Mrs. O. M. Butterfield as librarian in 1887, and is still in charge. Mr. A. is a native of New Albany, and was educated at Marengo Academy, in Crawford county and at DePauw college.

PUBLIC BUILDINGS.—In 1819 Seth Woodruff was paid $50 for building a "gaol" 12 feet square, with hewed logs 1 foot square, ceiling and floor to be also of hewed logs, and distance between floors 7 feet. Door 2 feet square, lined with iron.

This was the building in which Damon, the first man hung in New Albany, was confined. No guard was kept at this time, and a party of pioneers after rescuing a prisoner set fire to and burned the jail, and in May, 1823, the Commissioners "ordered that the house belonging to the estate of Joseph Brindley, on lot 31, Upper High street, be made use of for one year as a gaol." A subscription was circulated in 26, but the building of a permanent jail was postponed for lack of funds until 1829, when $300 was appropriated to build one, the "plan upon the ground to be 54x16 feet; criminal department 16 feet square, of hewn stone; remainder of said house, upon the ground and second story, to be for poor house and gaol keeper. The debtor's department to be immediately above the criminal. That building sufficed until the present substantial brick and stone structure was erected in 1858, under the superintendency of Isaac P. Smith, and which, with subsequent improvements cost the county about $15,000.

Court Houses.—Seth Woodruff, from New Jersey, located in New Albany shortly before Floyd county was organized, and erected a large frame tavern. Judge Woodruff is described as being a large framed, large brained, somewhat uncouth, but withal a kind-hearted man; who came west with a family, and plenty of surplus energy, physical strength, and go-aheaditiveness, which made his presence felt in the commuity. He was a man of force; Baptist preacher, tavern-keeper, brick-layer and in fact almost everything required in a new county. He served for many years as Justice of the Peace, Associate Judge, etc., his "picket fence" signature being a striking characteristic in the old county records. The first meeting of Commissioners was at Woodruff's tavern, on Main street, near east Fourth, and this was the headquarters for all county business, until the erection of a courthouse in 1823, excepting that the basement of the Presbyterian church was occupied for a short time.

The Scribners had donated the four corner lots at the crossing of Spring and State streets, for the purposes of the public. Upon one of these a court house was to be built, and New Albany's staunch business men had bound themselves to raise $9,000 for county buildings, when this village was made the county seat in 1819. Feb. 10, 20, it was "ordered that the Treasurer pay Wm. Norwood $10 for drawing a plan of the court house." "Ordered that the building of the court house and gaol be sold at public sale to the lowest bidder on the 3rd Monday in March." It was also "ordered that the above action be published in the *Indianian*, of Jeffersonville, the *Gazette*, of Corydon, and one notice be posted on Seth Woodruff's door." On the 20th of April, (a postponed date) the job was bid off by Charles Paxson and others, for $7,860. The contractors soon discovered, however, that they had taken the work too low and abandoned it. Subsequently the people complained regarding the inconveniences. The Commissioners brought suit against the bondsmen for the $9,000, and as steps were being taken to remove the county seat, the New Albanians opened a subscription to build a court house. The total raised was $3,256 00, which was thought to be enough to secure a fair sized court house. This building was occupied in November, 1824, but Seth Woodruff, who had subscribed $100 for a cupola and bell failed to complete his part of the agreement until 1827, the upper rooms having been completed the same year at a cost of $100 additional. The cost of that structure which was used for more than forty years as the seat of county justice was less than $3,000.

The present court house was erected 1855-7, of limestone from the Bedford quarries, and cost when completed $127,700. It is of Corinthian style, and equal to any county court house to be found in Indiana. The cornerstone was laid July 11, 60, with Masonic ceremonies. The building is 64x100, 40 feet in height, and fire proof.

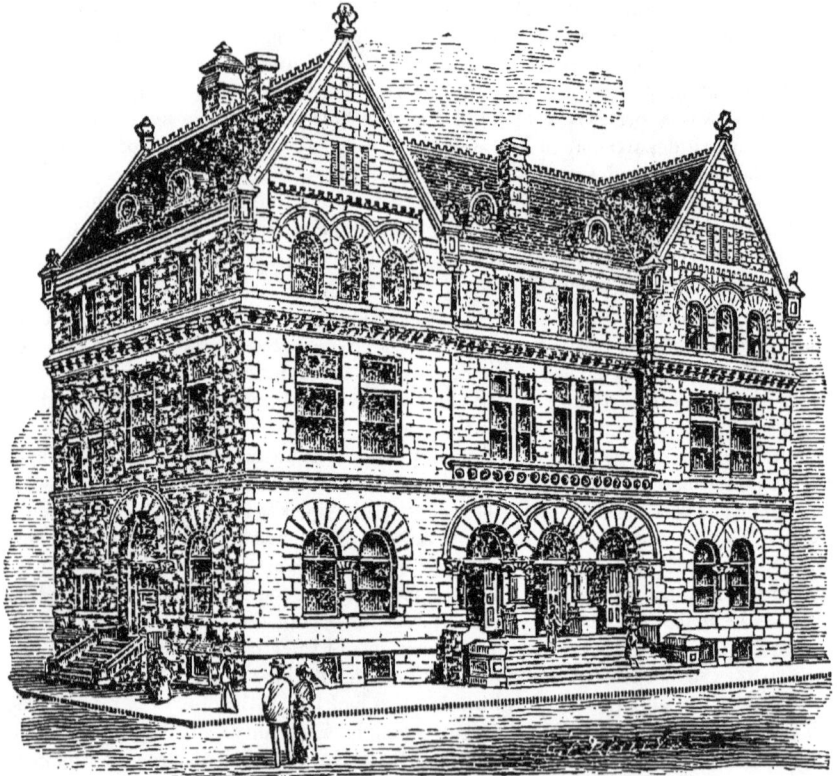

U. S. GOVERNMENT BUILDING.

The above handsome structure was commenced in 1886, and completed in 89. Judge Bicknell, while in Congress asked for $100,000, with which to erect a building, but the Act was not passed until 1884, under Congressman S. M. Stockslager, May 86. Capt. J. S. Neal, of Indianapolis, was appointed Superintendent of construction, Ben. F. Welker clerk, and J. B. Mitchell disbursing agent. Excavation commenced in June, and Anderson Brothers, of Findlay, Ohio, completed the foundation in 87. The carpenter work by John Mitchell, of Louisville, Ky., was completed in June, 88, and the finishing by Shover & Christian, in Nov. 88. Heating apparatus was put in about the same time by J. F. Dalton. The approaches were made by Crumbo & Melcher, and alley and sodding by J. R. Hatfield, the building having been turned over to the custodian Oct. 1, 88, at a total cost of about $100,000.

The building is handsome and commodious, being thoroughly adapted to all its present purposes, a credit to the Government and admired by all who see it.

POSTMASTERS.—The first postmaster in New Albany was Joel Scribner, succeeded in 1823 by his son Harvey Scribner. The Scribners erected a log hut which was used as a U. S. post office for several years. Succeeding the above came Gen. Alex. S. Burnett, 1836; Jno. W. Varnam, 41; Calvin W. Ruter, 45; Geo. H. Harrison, 49. P. M. Kent was appointed early in 53 but resigned after a few weeks service, and Frank Gwin succeeded. After Mr. Gwin's death Jan. 61, Wm. J. Newkirk served for 5 months, when John M. Wilson continued until D. W. Voyles came in 69. Maj. M. M. Hurley appointed January, 77, served under four administrations, and was removed by Cleveland in 85 under charges of being "a bitter republican partisan." Capt. John B. Mitchell was appointed in September 85, and served until July 89, within which period the government building was erected. The post-office was removed to its present commodious quarters October 1st. 88.

Walter B. Godfrey, the present Postmaster, was born in Luzerne county, Pa., April 17, 45, and graduated from the Blairstown Academy, in 1862. His father having been a manufacturer, he engaged in the same line, and in 73, became a superintendent at Lewistown, Pa., removing thence to New Albany in 77. For 12 years he was prominently identified with our manufactories. He was appointed P. M. July 1, 89, and commissioned Jan. 9, 90, for a four year's term. Mr. Godfrey has held the highest offices in the Masonic bodies here, and is prominent in social and political circles.

Geo. A. Newhouse, Jr, assistant P. M. is of German descent, a native of this city and educated in her public schools. Miss Carrie C. Claggett has charge of the money order and registry departments, which are kept open from 7:00 A. M. to 6:00 P. M. Jos. E. Lloyd is mailing clerk; Jno. W. Thompson, delivery clerk and Frank Sears, special delivery. Ten regular carriers and two extras are required in the free delivery system as follows: W. J. Thurman, H. F. Wells, O. P. Anderson, Thos. Maley, C. F. Green, C. M. Hatcher, Samuel Marsh, Jr., M. W. Sparks, W. E. Genung, Louis Meyer; and Harry Shipman and C. W. McFall as extras.

Ten regular mails are received daily and the same number dispatched, the aggregate of mail matter having steadily increased from year to year until at present about 250,000 pieces of first class mail is handled monthly and the entire force does not lack for employment. The force have systematized the work so that the average errors have been reduced to six per month, showing a very gratifying record.

INTERNAL REVENUE.—The 7th internal revenue district comprises 32 counties, and John F. Platt the traveling deputy collector is principally engaged in the fourth division of this district. Although born in Clarke county, he has been a resident of New Albany from infancy, was educated in the city schools and served in the drug trade for 8 years prior to his appointment, Dec. 17, 89, to the responsible position which he now holds. Mr. Platt was the republican candidate for city clerk, in 89, suffering the inevitable minority party defeat, with a reduced majority.

Mrs. Clara M. Wible, stamp deputy, is a native of this city. and graduate of the Female High School. She was appointed on the same day as the above.

U. S. COMMISSIONER.—James G. Harrison, who was appointed in 1890 as deputy clerk of U. S. Courts and commissioner, was born in Ohio, Sept. 29th, 34, removing with his parents to New Albany in 39. Educated in the city schools, he was appointed county recorder in 57, upon his father's death, and elected that fall, having ever since held some official position.

The Pension Board are Drs. W. H. Sheets, of Jeffersonville, president; A. M. Jones, of Corydon, secretary, and J. L. Stewart, of this city, treasurer.

CHARITABLE AND BENEVOLENT INSTITUTIONS.

County Poor House.—Formerly the poor, who were not kept at their homes, or in the county jail, were let by contract to some farmer, who was paid a small fee in addition to their labor; but in 1838 the county secured a farm of 140 acres 1½ miles north of the city. It contained a log house to which a log addition was added in 1842. About 1850, 167 acres was leased 3 miles north of the city. Afterward this was purchased and a frame house erected which answered the purposes of the county poor, until the present brick structure was built in 1878. This will comfortably accommodate 140 inmates, while the usual average is about 90. Mr. John Priestley is a native of England, came to this country in 1852, and has been in charge of the Alms house for 7 years past. Mr. Priestley is a man well adapted for the place. being a thorough going farmer, and a large portion of the supply for the table, comes from the products raised by the inmates, under his charge. He is ably assisted in the house management by his amiable wife, and everything is kept in the best possible condition, considering the mental and physical weakness, variety and social standing of their large family.

United Charities Hospital.—This institution was established Nov. 1888, in accordance with the munificent endowment of the late W. C. DePauw. and is under the management of a board of trustees consisting of 18 ladies. Six of these are chosen from the Centenary church, two from Wesley Chapel, and one each from other principal churches. Mr. DePauw was a man of great wealth, kind and generous, and determined that this city should receive many blessings. With this end in view, after leaving 40 per cent. of the residue of his estate to the DePauw University, at Greencastle, and 5 per cent. to the DePauw College, of this city, he bequeathed an additional 5 per cent. for the purposes of this association, which are; "the keeping of a free reading room, establishing and maintaining an industrial school, a dispensary, infirmary, general hospital, lying-in hospital, home for the friendless, bath rooms, and a coffee and sandwich room, agreeably in all respects to the provisions and directions of said will." The four-story brick building at Nos. 82, 84 and 86, E. Main street, is in use, and under the provisions of the will, the amount available for improvements will increase from year to year. The public were slow to appreciate the benefits to be secured in this charitable institution; but the admissions are constantly on the increase, now averaging about 15 per month. The present number of patients is not far from 20 and the building will comfortably accommodate four times that number. Miss Eva Ola Smith, a native of this city, has been matron since the institution was opened, and presides with grace and dignity. This institution is destined to confer a great blessing upon the poor and unfortunate, and will be a greater monument to its sympathetic donor than columns of granite, extending to the sky, could be.

Cornelia Memorial Orphans Home.—Mr. Woodward gave the use of a building for this purpose, and a home was opened on the corner of Main and Third streets, March 18, 77. A few years later Mr. DePauw donated the use of a building located at Spring and Third, and the home was moved there, where it remained until 82. Finding that the inmates were increasing so that it would be necessary to secure additional room, Mr. Culbertson purchased an acre of ground on Ekin Avenue and erected the present brick building, which with the school building adjoining covers about one-third of the lot. He made a free gift of this for the purposes of the orphans home, and it was named Cornelia Memorial in memory of his deceased wife. The building will conveniently accommodate 60 inmates, there being now an average of from 45 to 50. Arrangements have been made to give ten months schooling, yearly. The home is situated in a beautiful high and healthful place, and there has been only 5 deaths at this institution in the past 15 years. Mrs. Mary McClane, matron, is a native of New York and came to New Albany in 53. She has been in the home, as matron, since its organization in 77, and is assisted by her daughter, Miss Alice. Every department of the home is kept in first class condition, and the institution is in high favor among our citizens, who greatly appreciate the generosity of Mr. Culbertson and the successful management of this charitable establishment.

The Old Ladies Home.—In 1873, W. S. Culbertson erected a building at a cost of $25,000, which was located on Main street, opposite Upper Seventh, designed for the benefit of needy and worthy widows. He has made provision for its future maintainance; by a liberal endowment fund. The building will comfortably accommodate from twenty-five to thirty persons. It has 20 rooms and is located on a high, dry and healthful place. There have been only 25 deaths in the 19 years since its organization. It is a non-sectarian institution, and the only qualification required is a good moral character, without a home, and unable to support themselves. Miss Mary Baldwin, who has been matron of the Old Ladies Home, since its organization, is a native of Kentucky, and came to New Albany in 53. Everything is kept scrupulously neat and clean, and the old ladies in their last days, without the usual home or friends, are made as comfortable as it is possible for human thoughtfulness to make them.

Cemeteries.—Formerly a "grave yard" was located on Lower First street, east of Spring, but after the opening of the Northern Burial Ground, about 1842, this place became popular as a resting place for the dead, and a few years later, the remains were largely removed from the W. First street grounds and the location abandoned as a cemetery. The Northern Burial Ground is owned by the city and since Oct. 15, 91, has been under control of a board of regents: Dr. S. C. Wilcox, Pres.; E. M. Hubbert, V. P.: H. A. Goetz, Sec.; G. W. Smith, Treas.; T. E. Austin, Moses Irwin and Geo. A. Newhouse, Sr. M. C. Baily, Supt., has charge of selling lots, improvements, etc., and gives employment to several men in the care and beautifying of the place. Mr. Baily is a native of Ky., and was appointed to the charge of the New Albany cemetery Nov. 91. Ed. Summers cemetery Clk. The area of the cemetery covers 74 acres, contains numerous vaults and handsome monuments, and has had about 10,500 burials.

The New Albany National Cemetery was established Dec. 15, 62. Within its walls sleep over 2,850 soldiers of the late war. It is located on a high eminence, fronting 370 ft. on Ekin av. extending back 730 ft. and containing about $5\frac{1}{2}$ acres. John Laun, the superintendent, is a native of Germany; served in the late war; was appointed superintendent of the New Jersey Natl. Cemetery June 2, 84, and transferred to his present charge Feb. 23, 89.

The Catholic congregations each have a burial ground –that of Holy Trinity church being located on the Green Valley road, near the city limits, and the St. Marys cemetery on the Charlestown road, near head of Vincennes street.

There is also a colored burying ground on West street, near Ealy.

BANKING INTERESTS.—It is seldom you can find a city of this size, that employs less outside capital than New Albany, in its various enterprises. Our five banks are backed by an abundant capital, which are largely the results of profitable investments in the industrial pursuits of this place. The officers and stockholders of

these, having made their money in New Albany are willing to encourage manufacturing enterprises and have abundance of home capital for every legitimate pursuit.
The banking interests of a community are of great importance to the general welfare.
and the standing of the men at the head of these institutions is a matter which concerns every person in the city. We can confidently refer to the banking officers of
this place as a strictly reliable, conservative and enterprising set of men. The banks
are backed by ample capital and are judiciously managed. This condition of matters
adds largely to the commercial and manufacturing stability of New Albany, and fail-
ures, by men of any reasonable ability, have been very rare indeed.

First National Bank..—The predecessors of this organization began business
in New Albany as a branch of the State Bank of Indiana, in 1834. Mason C. Fitch
was first president, and James Shields cashier. Three years later the substantial
stone bank building, now occupied, on the corner of Main and Bank streets, was
erected at a cost of about $50,000, and which remained for many years as the costli-
est building in New Albany. The stone was taken from a quarry on the knobs, and
its exposure for more than half a century has demonstrated that it will stand the rav-
ages of time, practically unchanged. The capital stock of this bank was increased to
$200,000 about Jan. 1833, and at the expiration of its charter in 1851, it paid a hand-
some dividend to its stockholders, and was merged into the Bank of the State of Indiana. With the changes of the banking system, in 1865, this institution again made
a satisfactory settlement with its stockholders, and formed the First National Bank,
Jesse J. Brown, president, and Walter Mann, cashier. When the bank was reorganized in 84, Mr. Brown declined the presidency and became vice president. while W.
S. Culbertson, who had been a director since 1840, was chosen as president. Mr.
Culbertson was born at New Market, Pa., in 1814. When 15 years of age he secured employment in a dry goods house at Harrisburg, where he remained with the firm
for five years, and in 1835 came to New Albany, where he engaged as clerk in the
dry goods store of Gen. A. S. Burnett, corner of Main and Pearl streets. He was 40
years in mercantile trade, 30 years of which in wholesale, and has been variously
connected with manufacturing enterprises.

Samuel A. Culbertson from early boyhood, has been trained to the banking
business. Beginning as a messenger in 1880, he was soon promoted to teller, and
was elected cashier July 14, 84. His six years of satisfactory service speaks for itself.
John A. Hutton who has been connected with the bank for 8 years, has officiated as
assistant cashier for 4 years past. The capital stock of this bank is $300,000, and its
surplus and undivided profits $100,000. The directors are W. S. Culbertson, J. J.
Brown, A. Dowling, M. McDonald and J. K. Woodard, jr., all men of high financial
and social standing.

The New Albany Banking Company.—Capital stock, $100,000; surplus,
$20,000. This institution was chartered by the Legislature of Indiana February, 1832,
under the title of the New Albany Insurance Company, and had been in continuous
business, from 1832 under that title, until April, 1877, when by order of the Floyd
Circuit Court, the word insurance was changed to banking, and the institution still
continues its business under the changed name of the New Albany Banking Company.
Elias Ayres and Harvey Scribner were its first president and secretary in 1832. The
charter of this company was granted for seventy-five years with full and broad powers
of insurance and banking, with the privilege of charging any rate of interest or dis-

count that might be agreed upon, not to exceed fifty per cent. The late John B. Winstandley became connected with the institution many years ago, and remained with it until his death in 1884, during which time he was its president. Isaac S. Winstandley, the son of John B. Winstandley, has also been connected with the institution since 1857 as secretary and cashier, and succeeded his father as president in 1884. Mr. I. S. Winstandley, the president of the company, has been closely identified with the city's progressive development, having been variously engaged in banking and manufacturing, and has been a promoter of many of the leading enterprises of New Albany and Louisville. He was a member of the board of school trustees from April 73, until June 79, and was very largely instrumental in placing our schools on a good foundation. He was also connected with the Kentucky and Indiana Bridge Company, during its construction, as a director, secretary and treasurer, resigning these positions after the completion of the bridge. He was also a director and a member of the executive committee of the board of directors, of the Louisville, New Albany and Chicago Railroad during 1890 and 1891.

Clarence J. Frederick, secretary and cashier of the company, is a native of this place, graduated from the New Albany Business College in 1876, and served as deputy county treasurer for six years. He commenced business with the New Albany Banking Company as bookkeeper, Jan. 1, 1882, and two years later was promoted to his present responsible position.

The pedigree of each share of stock in the New Albany Banking Company, can be traced through the books to the date of its original subscription. Dividends have been regularly declared to its stockholders since its organization- the last cash dividend of Jan. 1, 1892, being number 73.

The continuous prosperity of this organization, through its successive changes, speaks well for New Albany enterprises and financial tact. The present directors are G. C. Cannon, Paul Reising, W. L. Breyfogle, E. L. Hurrle, I. S. Winstandley, John H. Stotsenburg and W. C. Winstandley. The bank is located at the corner Pearl and Market streets.

New Albany National.—This bank was organized on Jan. 4. 1865, with capital stock of $200,000, and has regularly declared semi-annual dividends of 5 per cent. besides making an annual addition to its surplus. The capital was largely increased at one time, but later was reduced to its original amount, of $200,000, at which it still remains, while the surplus and undivided profits add $110,000 to the aggregate. The bank was first situated at the corner of Pearl and Main streets, removing to the present location, at No. 15, E. Main, after the purchase of this block in 1869. J. M. Hains was elected as president at the beginning of the organization and still continues in that capacity. He is in the milling business under which heading will be found his personal mention. M. A. Weir was born at Salem, Ind., Dec. 2, 1827, and has been variously connected in commercial and manufacturing pursuits. He was one of the organizers, and cashier of the First National Bank of Mt. Vernon for 8 years. In 1874 he assisted in the organization of the Second National Bank of this city, continuing as its cashier from 1874 to 1882, and upon the resignation of H. A. Scribner as cashier of the New Albany National bank Dec. 25th, 84. Mr. Weir at once assumed his present position. He also assisted in the organization of the Citizens Bank at Salem, Oct., 89, of which he is vice president and a director. W. P. Brewer, is a native of Martingsburg, Ind.; has been connected with this bank for 6 years past, and

24 . DESCRIPTIVE SKETCH

assistant cashier since Jan. 91. Salem P. Town who was county clerk 1853-61, has for 10 years past, had charge of the individual ledger, and A. D. Brewer, a brother of the assistant cashier, keeps the general ledger. The present directors are N. T. DePauw, C. W. DePauw, John McCulloch, J. M. Hains, Peter R. Stoy, Moses Irwin and M. A. Weir.

From its organization the New Albany National Bank, has maintained a high position as a financial institution and its stockholders have had no reason to be dissatisfied with the returns. It is backed by ample capital judiciously managed and carries the usual line of deposits.

The Merchants National.—This monetary institution was established Jan. 6, 65. Its officers were Gen. A. S. Burnett, president; James R. Shields, cashier; and the above with Lawrence Bradley, J. Hangary and R. G. McCord were its directors. The Merchants National was first established on Main street, between Pearl and Bank, and remained there until the purchase of the present location, corner of Pearl and Main. The brick building on this corner was destroyed by fire in 68, and the bank erected the present structure at a cost of $12.500. The capital stock was originally $200,000, but Feb. 23, 78. was reduced to $100,000, and when it was reorganized at the expiration of its 20 years of charter, it was made a non-dividend declaring bank. N. T. DePauw, president. is also president of the Glass Works, and will be mentioned in an article on that subject. E. C. Hangary, cashier, is a native of this city, was educated in the Philadelphia schools, and returned to New Albany in 1863. He commenced as bookkeeper in the Merchants National Bank Sept. 74, and was promoted to the responsible position of cashier in May 75. Mr. Hangary served as secretary of the Water Works for 8 years. from 83 to 91, and has been connected with different manufacturing enterprises of this vicinity. J. Hangary Fawcett. assistant cashier, is a native of New Albany, received his education in the city schools, and engaged in this bank six years ago, 2 years since accepting his present position. The directors are as follows: N. T. DePauw, C. W.DePauw, J. K, Woodward, Jr., I. P. Leyden, C. H. Fawcett and E. C. Hangary. Officered as above with several of New Albany's stanchest business men. The Merchants National Bank carries a popular line of deposits averaging about $300,000, and is annually making a satisfactory addition to its accumulations, while it affords perfect security to its depositors.

Second National.—Notwithstanding the fact that the banking capital of New Albany aggregated a million dollars, some of the citizens here, early in 1874, believed that a fifth bank could be successfully established, and after considerable efforts the capital stock of $100,000 was secured, and the Second National Bank chartered n August 1874. Lawrence Bradley was chosen president; J. F. Butler, vice president; M. A. Weir, cashier, and the above, with R. G. McCord and R. P. Main, made up the directors. The present officers are Lawrence Bradley, president, who has continued in this capacity since the organization of the bank. Mr. Bradley is also president of the Cotton Batting mills under which article he will have personal mention. E. B. Lapping. cashier, is a native of this city; educated in New Albany public schools and at the academy, under charge of Profs. Morse and May. Mr. Lapping accepted a position in the Second National in 1878, and in 1884 was promoted to the cashiership. L. L. Bradley, assistant cashier. is a native of this city, son of the president, and was educated in the same schools as Mr. Lapping. The directors are L. Bradley, E. B. Lapping, C. P. Cook. Jas. Andrews, R. P. Main, S. W. Waltz and Jacob Goodbub.

The surplus and undivided profits of this bank is above $35,000, which with capital stock, and average deposits of about $175,000 make a sufficient amount to meet the requirements of its numerous customers.

THE PRESS.—The opinions of the people are largely moulded by the newspapers; and to enterprising journals the progress of a city is often due. The press of New Albany has generally held an honorable reputation and ever been ready to advocate measures designed for the upbuilding of the place. The journals here at the present time are of a high local character.

Ebenezer Patrick started a paper in New Albany in the fall of 1820, which continued for a year or two, and the Microscope begun April, 17, 24, in Louisville, was moved to this place, September of that year, by Dr. T. H. Roberts. This continued only a year. The Cresent and the Aurora were each started within the next 5 years, but soon succumbed.

Whig and Republican Papers.—In Nov. 1830, Collins Brothers commenced the Gazette which, with changing proprietors and under the names of Gazette, Bulletin, Commercial and Tribune, continued a succession until about 1870. In 37, Thos. Collins issued the Gazette as a daily. Besides Collins we find the name of Mattingly, Wm. Green, Leonard Green, Barnett and others connected with the above papers. In 52 Collins & Green sold out to Milton Gregg, who was later assisted by his sons. Several of the Gregg family died 56-7, and after suspension for a time, J. P. Hancock undertook to revive the paper but with indifferent success. During the greater part of the war no republican paper was printed here, but through the efforts of J. P. Luse and Schuyler & Harriott the Commercial was started in 64. It was sold to H. N. Gifford, who continued it for several years, but finding that it was an unprofitable investment the paper was discontinued. When it suspended the material and franchises were bought by the Ledger company. For a number of years succeeding, the republicans of Floyd county depended principally upon the Louisville Commercial for political precept. About 1870, Mr. Keiger started the second Tribune, which run for a short time. McPheeters & Bradbury started the New Albany Republican in 1880, which was well printed but only lived a year or two. April 16, 88, Packard & Brown were induced to start the

Daily and Weekly Tribune.—Jan. 1, 89, a stock company was formed with Jasper Packard, president, and John W. Edmondson, secretary and treasurer. The Tribune press is run by an electric motor, and the office fitted for commercial job work. Having lived four years with increasing prosperity, it has passed the experimental stage and is on a good foundation for continued success. Hon. Jasper Packard, editor and manager of the Tribune, was born in Mahoning county, O., Feb. 23, his parents moving to Indiana three years later. Mr. Packard graduated in the classical department of the Michigan University 1855, settling in Laporte the next year, where he read law, and was admitted to the bar in 60. The next year he enlisted as a private in the Union army, and through meritorious services held the rank of Colonel and Brevet Brig. Gen., when discharged in 1866. Gen. Packard succeeded Schuyler Colfax in Congress, holding the position 3 successive terms. In 1874 he established the Laporte Chronicle, conducting it until he accepted the position of Internal Revenue Agent, in 1876, subsequent to which he was again engaged in the newspaper business at Laporte prior to coming to New Albany. J. W. Edmondson, who has been with the Tribune from its commencement, is a native of this city, and for many years was engaged in the produce commission business.

Democratic and other Journals.—The Argus was started in 36, by Dennison & Hineline as a democratic paper. This was purchased in 38 by Hutchens & Thompson, the former selling his interest to Virder a few months later. Thompson continued with this paper till it was suspended in 41. J. C. Joycelyn issued the Register for 2 years, but in 44 the plant was purchased by P. M. Kent, and the name changed to the Democrat. Kent shortly afterwards sold to C. D. Hineline and in 45 Bradley and Lucas were proprietors. Norman & Morrison purchased the plant in 46, and Sept. 1, 49, Norman, Morrison & Mathews commenced the

Daily Ledger.—Mr. Norman continued as editor and one of the proprietors until his death, Oct. 30, 1869, when his interest was purchased by L. G. Matthews, who in June 72, transferred the plant to Merrill & Moter, and two months later it was consolidated with the Standard, which had been started July 31, 71; the new issue taking the name of the Ledger-Standard. Since the above consolidation extensive additions have been made to the plant from time to time, the job department fitted with modern faced type, necessary machinery put in and a good bindery established, making the Ledger one of the most complete offices in Southern Indiana. August 15, 81, the Standard was dropped from the name leaving it as originally started in 49, the Daily and Weekly Ledger.

Captain Jonathan Peters the manager of the Ledger Company is a native of Orange County, Indiana, was commissioned as 2d Lieutenant of Co. F, 117 Ind. Vols. in Aug. 63. He was in active service in the Cumberland mountains during the winter campaign of 63-4 as quartermaster of the 117th regiment. For several years subsequent to the war Captain Peters was a Commercial Agent, but in Nov. 72, he purchased an interest in the Ledger-Standard and was elected as president of the company, a position which he has now held for nearly twenty years.

James P. Applegate purchased an interest in the Ledger-Standard in 72 and has been connected with it ever since. For 11 years past he has occupied the position of editor. Mr. Applegate was born in Jeffersonville, educated in the free schools and at Indiana University. He held the office of Recorder of Clark county eight years. Was very active in politics and generally held official positions on committees. He represented Floyd, Clark and Jefferson counties in the legislature of 1889, the body which passed the new election laws, the school book law and others of general interest, and the act creating a board of sinking fund commissioners, of especial interest to New Albany. He takes a deep interest in streets and park tree planting in the city and his efforts in this direction are apparent on the streets of the city.

Charles W. Cottom who has been in newspaper business in New Albany since 1850, has charge of the local department of the Ledger, and is thoroughly posted on the history of the city.

Saturday Herald.—This paper started in 75 as an advertising medium, with free distribution, and five years later was purchased by J. W. Conner who has published it for a dozen years with good success. Several thousand copies are printed each week and the office is fitted for commercial printing of all kinds. Mr. Conner also conducts a wall paper and book store near the corner of Pearl and Spring streets, in connection with the printing business.

The Public Press was commenced June 22, 81, by Josiah Gwin, who 10 years prior had been the chief spirit in starting the Standard, remaining with the consolidated Ledger-Standard until Feb. 14, 84, when he sold his interest to Jno. B. Mitchell. Mr. Gwin is a native of Harrison county, educated in the city schools, learned the printer's art, served as county recorder from 61 to 70, and has since then been almost continuously engaged in the printing business. The Public Press is democratic; is well equipped and conveniently located at No. 67, Pearl street.

A German paper was started in 1850, which lived but a short time, and a second one in 61 met with a similar fate. The Deutsche Zeitung started June 28, 75, by Otto Palmer survived for several years. Other German and English papers have been started but were short lived.

John R. Nunemacher Co.—Although this house prints no regular journal, transient publications, of any desirable size or shape, are produced, and everything in commercial, book and job printing comes in its line. John R. Nunemacher, deceased, was for many years connected with the book trade of this city, and in 1871 opened a printing office in connection therewith. The latter department rapidly increased, at length became the principal feature, and the book business was discontinued. New presses, other machinery and material have been added from time to time until this is now among the best fitted job printing offices in New Albany, turning out all kinds of printing with promptness, and in the best style of the art. Ten to twelve hands are given employment, the work of the office going largely to New Albany firms. Walter C. Nunemacher, manager, is a native of this city, educated in our public schools and in 1871 commenced the printers trade in this office, a few years later becoming foreman and on the decease of his father in 1882, he succeeded to the management of the business, at No. 40 E. Main Street. Mr. Nunemacher has been an active worker for the upbuilding of the city, having succeeded N. T. DePauw as president of the Commercial Club, which position he filled with honor until the election of the present incumbent, Judge Cardwill. He is treasurer of the Young Men's Christian Association and the building committee of the same. He is also a director in the New Albany Clothing Company.

Home Organizer.—The latest venture in New Albany journalism is the Home Organizer which made its first appearance Feb. 13, of the present year. It is an advertising sheet, with free distribution, and advocates the cause of the labor unions. It is published by J. G. Ewing & Co. at 65, State street, and edited by Miss Belle E. Pierson, who is a vigorous champion of the labor cause. The success of the Home Organizer, in its commencing weeks, has met the expectations of its projectors.

CHURCHES, ETC.—Including the German and A. M. E. organizations, there are 8 Methodist churches in New Albany, 3 Presbyterian, 2 Christian, 3 Baptist, including colored, 2 Catholic, and 1 each of Episcopal, German Evangelical, Second Advent, which together with the Y. M. C. A., and other religious organizations furnish the foundation for a highly moral community. The white Methodists of this city number 2,250 regular communicants; the Presbyterians 1,350; Catholic 950 families, and other denominations as reported under their respective heads.

METHODIST EPISCOPAL CHURCHES.

Wesley Chapel.—Rev. John Shrader organized a class of the M. E. church at the residence of Mrs. Ruff in 1817, and on Nov. 25th of that year dedicated the first church building of this place. In 1830, the brick building, now rear part of Dr. Knoeful's drug store was erected which served the church, as a house of worship, for 24 years. The building on Market, below W. 2d, was solidly constructed in 1854, requiring 552,000 hard brick in its erection. Together with lot and parsonage the church property is valued at $25,500. Wesley Chapel gives convenient accommodations for its membership of nearly 500 regular communicants, and Sabbath school of 375 members. The latter organization, a short intermission excepted, has been under the superintendency of Peter R. Stoy for the past 40 years.

The pastors prior to 1838 were Revs. Shrader, Lecke, McReynolds, Davis, Wiley, Thompson, Goode, and Lowe. J. C. Smith came in 38; Wm. Knowles, 39; W. V. Daniels, 40; Silas Rawson, 41; G. C. Beeks, 42; E. C. Wood, 43; F. C. Holliday, 45; Jas. Hills, 47; W. C. Smith, 49; H. Gilmore, 50; Jas. H Noble, 52; J. Y. McKee, 54; B. F. Crarey, 56; Sam'l Reed, 57. S. B. Sutton, 58; J. M. Green, 60; Hayden Hayes, 62; Noble again in 64; W. McK. Hester, 67; Stephen Bowers, 70, Aaron Turner, 71; Jos. S. Woods, 72; Wm. H. Grim, 74; J. L. Pitner, 77; Woods again, 80; A. R. Julian, 83; T. H. Willis, 86, and the Rev. E. R. Vest 91. Rev. Vest is a native of Scott county, Ind., studied theology and classics at the DePauw University of Greencastle, Ind., graduating from there in 85, and preaching at Spencer, Mooresville and Martinsville, prior to coming here.

Centenary M. E.—The old Foundry in London was opened by Methodism in 1739, and 100 years later, the New Albany, Centenary M. E. church was erected. Subsequent to that date the First church has been known as Wesley Chapel. The building on Spring street above E. 31, has been remoddled somewhat, but stands essentially as it was erected more than half a century ago.

The pastors have been J. C. Smith, 39; Wm. Knowles, 41; Silas Rawson, 42; R. Robinson, 43; Isaac Crawford, 45; Allen Wiley, 47; T. H. Rucker, 49; W. Terrill 51; C. B. Davidson, 53; B. F. Rawlins, 54; S. J. Gillett, 56. T. H. Lynch, 57; D. McIntire, 58; Elijah Fletcher 60; R. L. Cushman' 61; N. P. Heth, 64; Jas. Hill, 66; H. R. Naylor, 69; S. L. Binkley, 72; J. S. Woods, 74; W. F. Harned, 76; Jas. Dixon, 77; Geo. D. Watson, 78; E. T. Curnick, 80; H. J. Talbott, 83; John Poucher 84; Talbott again, 86, and Rev. J. E. Steele, since Sept. 88. Rev. Steele is a native of Carroll county, Ind., graduated from DePauw University in 86, preaching in Indianapolis 2 years prior to coming here. The present membership of Centenary church is over 500. Value of church property about $15,000. C. P. Gwin is Superintendent of Sabbath school.

Trinity and John Street.—Mr. John Conner donated a corner lot on E. 11th street, and the John's street M. E. church was organized and a building erected in 57. The pastors have been Wm. B. Mason, J. H. Ketcham, Jos. Wharton, Lee Welker, B. F. Tarr, Geo. Telle, Chas. Cross, J. J. Hite, John Julian, J. H. Clippinger, G. F. Culmer, Wm. McK. Hester. T. D. Welker, F. C. Iglehart, H. J. Talbott, 74; H. N. King, 75; F. Walker, 77; E. T. Curnick, 78; Walter Underwood, 80; Walker again, 82; St. Claire, 83; Byron Carter, 85; F. J. Mallett, 87-8. About this time the John's street congregation principally united with the new Trinity organization, but still holds its trustees and legal separate existence. J. V. Givler, was pastor for a time, succeeded by Dr. John Poucher, 89, and Rev. Talbott was for the fourth time returned to a New Albany charge in Sept. 89. Born in Greencastle, Ind., Mr. Talbott graduated from the DePauw University, of his native town in 73, since which he has been in the ministry, and having had other charges here is favorably known by New Albany people. The Trinity church building corner Spring and 13th streets was erected in 89, and cost with lot about $40,000. The present membership is about 400. W. D. Keyes superintends the Sabbath school and Prof. B. A. May is president of the Epworth League.

Main Street M. E.—This church was organized about 1850, having been named ed Roberts Chapel at the start in honor of Bishop Roberts. The present brick edifice on Main, below W. 5th st., was erected in 1877, and with lot is worth about $4,000. The membership is about 300. The pastors so far as we have been able to obtain them have been prior to the close of the war, Revs. Kerns, Coffin, Daniels, Cross, Clark, Cushman, and following these, S. L. Binkley, 65; G. W. Bowers, 68; Carson, Tarr, 69; B. Carter, 70; John Tansy, 71; H. J. Barr, 72; John Spears, 74; J. W. Culmer, 76; J. W. McCormick, 77; S. W. McNaughton, 79; John Walls, 80; J. W. Julian, 82; G. W, Fansler, 84; J. W. Payne, 87; W. S. Rader, 88. Rev. W. S. Biddle, the present incumbent, is a native of Indianapolis, and graduated from DePauw University in 86, coming from the charge at Grandview to the Main street church Sept. 89. The Sabbath school with 200 regular attendants is in charge of Thos. Plaiss.

German M. E.—A class of German Methodists was formed about 1850, meeting for several years in one of the public school buildings. The brick church on 5th st., near Market, was dedicated in 1864, and served as a place of worship until the handsome edifice, at the corner of E. Fifth and Spring, was erected in 1889-90. This with furnishing, lot and parsonage, cost fully $20,000. The names of the pastors so far as we have been able to obtain them, are Revs. Heller, Muth, Brunig, Doerr, Ruff, Lich, A. Klein, 75; C, Golder, 77; G. Treftz, 79; J. C. Weidman, 80; C. G. Fritche, 81; H. Grentzenberg, 82; C. G. Herzer, 85; and J. F. Severinghaus, 87, who is a native of Germany, a self-educated homeopathic physician, and is now on his fifth year as pastor of the above church. Present membership 180.

Jennie DePauw Memorial.—Epaphras Jones, who owned the lands in the vicinity of Vincennes street, before the Scribners came to New Albany, about 1820, undertook to build a rival town, calling his plat Providence. In 1850, Mrs. F. Graham opened a Sunday school in her home on Vincennes street, and a year later, the Methodists erected a mission chapel. The building of the John's street church in 57, drew away from this and for some time no services were held on Vincennes street. In 1865, the late Hon. W. C. DePauw purchased from the Lutherans the building formerly occupied as the Episcopal church, and moved it to Vincennes street, where it was long known as the Kingsley mission. This was burned in 83, and Mr. DePauw at once erected the present building. Just as it was ready for dedication, Jennie DePauw, aged 13 years, died, and in memory of the daughter of one who has contributed more to Methodist enterprises than any other man of his time, the new building was named as above, Nov. 3, 1884. The class started with six members, T. S. Hynes pastor, but at the end of the year had 125 enrolled. H. J. Barr was pastor in 85; G. W. Fansler, 86; W. McK. Hester, 87, continuing for 4 years. Rev. Hester is a native of Clark county, and in the ministry since 1850. Rev. S. L. Niles, succeeded as pastor at the last session of Conference.

Rev. J. M. Baxter, a native of Ohio, who has been a member of the Indiana Conference for 18 years past, was made Presiding Elder of the New Albany district in 1889. This charge covers 6 stations and 16 circuits, representing Floyd, Harrison and Washington counties, and a portion of Orange and Crawford, the P. E. having executive powers and general charge over the above territory with headquarters in New Albany.

PRESBYTERIAN CHURCHES.

The Scribners were of the Presbyterian persuasion, although tolerant towards all evangelical churches. Not having enough of that sect in New Albany to organize a church, on Feb. 16, 1816, Mrs. Phoebe Scribner, with her children, Joel, James and Esther, united with Thomas Posey, (later Governor of Indiana,) his wife, John Gibson and wife, and J. M. Tunstall, to form the Union church, at Jeffersonville. Shortly afterwards Mary Meriwether and Mary Wilson were added, but as the members had scattered, and the Scribners were the principal support, a meeting was held Dec. 7, 1817, at the residence of Phoebe Scribner, now the central portion of the Commercial hotel, when the church was reorganized by Rev. Banks, of Louisville, into the

First Presbyterian church of New Albany, with Phoebe, Joel, James, Esther and Mary Scribner, Jacob Marcell and wife and Stephen Beers and wife, as the membership. Rev. Isaac Reed came in Sept. 1818, remaining for 15 months. In the fall of 19, a frame church, 30x40 ft was erected, which burned down 2 years later. A Sabbath school started about this time by Mrs. Nathaniel Scribner and Catherine Silliman, was reputed to have been the first in Indiana. Ezra H. Day was pastor from Oct., 22, till his death in Sept., 23. J. T. Hamilton preached each alternate week from 24 to 28, receiving a salary of $160 a year, half of which was contributed by Elias Ayers. Ashbel S. Wells came in 28, and under his ministrations a hundred new members were added and a brick church was erected on State near Spring which was dedicated Feb. 26, 30. S. K. Sneed became pastor in June, 32; W. C. Anderson, 38; F. S. Howe, 43; Dan'l Stewart 44; J. M. Stevenson, 49; T. E. Thomas, 57; R. L. Breck, 58; J. P. Safford, 62; Anderson again, 67; Samuel Conn, 70, and Rev. J. W. Clokey commenced his services here July 7, 1878. Rev. Clokey is a native of Jefferson county, Ohio; graduated from Wittenberg college, of Springfield, Ohio, in 59; studied theology at Xenia, and has been in the ministry since 1863, removing from Middletown, O., to this charge, in which he has labored for nearly 14 years.

The commodious church on Bank, between Main and Market streets, was erected 1852-4, and with lot and furnishings cost about $35,000. The present membership is about 300. A flourishing Sunday school in connection is superintended by Samuel W. Vance, and the Main street mission school in charge of J. F. Gebhart.

Second Presbyterian.—From various reasons, shortly after the series of annual camp meetings was commenced by Sneed and others at Mt. Tabor, a division of the First church occurred and the Second was organized 1837 with Rev. Sneed as pastor. This church united with the New School Presbytery. The congregation met for worship in the court house for a time, later using the female seminary building on E. 4th street. The church building, erected by the Second, corner Main and E. Third, cost $24,500, and was dedicated Aug. 1, 52. At that time it was the handsomest church edifice in the city. A year or two since it was sold to the colored Baptists, for $6,000. The present superb edifice, corner Elm and 13th streets, was dedicated Dec. 14, 90. This structure with lot cost $35,000. The seating capacity is about 600, and when lecture room is added by opening the folding doors, at least 1,100 persons can be accommodated. Membership above 300.

The ministers in charge have been S. K. Sneed, 37; E. R. Beadle, 43; John Black,

45; J. M. Bishop, 46; D. Stewart, 50; J. G. Atterbury, 51; H. C. Hovey, 66; Stewart again, 69; Rev. Dickson, 72; Chas. Little, 76; Wm. Goodloe, 80: W. L. Austin, 84, and Rev. D. Vandyke, who has been in charge since Sept. 89. Rev. Vandyke is a native of Ohio; an alumnus of Lane seminary and has been in the ministry for 30 years. The society is now erecting a handsome parsonage, of modern architectural design, adjoining the church, which with lot will cost about $7,500. The Sabbath school is under the superintendency of C. H. Conner. For 20 years past a mission school has also been conducted at West Union.

Third Presbyterian.—The growth of the city and Second church made it desirable to have another place of worship, and on Oct. 31, 53, 24 members withdrew from the Second to organize the Third church. A lot had been donated by the heirs of Judge Conner, and a church building erected as a mission chapel, corner of Oak and 9th, prior to the separation. The organization prospered and Feb. 9, 68, the substantial stone building, corner of Spring and 9th streets, costing $26,000 was dedicated. Rev. Chas. Hutchinson has served the church as pastor since its organization, 38½ years ago, and by his zealous and consistent Christian character, has endeared himself, not only to his own flock of over 750 members, but to all good citizens of New Albany. Rev. Hutchinson was born at Norwich, Vt., July 15, 1820; graduated from Dartmouth college in 43, and from Andover theological seminary 3 years later. A Sunday school of over 400 is under the charge of Silas D. Loughmiller. A church building was erected at Mt. Tabor in 1838, and a society maintained there for about 15 years, but it was disbanded about the time of the organization of the Third church, its membership largely coming to their society. A Sabbath school and preaching is maintained at Mt. Tabor, 3 miles north, and also at McCulloch chappel, 3 miles east. Rev. Hutchinson is a well preserved man for one of his years, but the charge is so large that he needs an assistant.

First Baptist.—Nicholas Storch began preaching the doctrines of the Baptist church, in Germany, about the year 1520, and the Anabaptist sect, as the society was first known, was formed at about the same time Luther started the Reformation.

Seth Woodruff, who has been mentioned elsewhere, organized a Baptist church in New Albany, about 1825. After 10 years, dissentions arose which led to a division, 43 members going to form Park Christian church, and in 1844 a second Baptist church was formed. After several propositions to unite the two Baptist churches had failed, the better element from these formed what is now the First Baptist church of New Albany, May 11, 1848. The same year its members erected the brick structure which still stands at corner Bank and Spring streets. The old First continued its organization until 1878, when its principal members united with the present organization. The church building on E. Fourth near Market, was erected in 1879, and cost with lot about $8,000. Dr. J. W. Juett is superintendent of S. S,, and Dr. J. L. Stewart has served as church clerk for 20 years. The present membership is about 350.

The following pastors have served the church in the order named: Revs. Armstrong, Geo. Giry, G. F. Pentecost, Harry Smith, W. M. Pratt, D. D., T. P. Campbell, J. C. Burkhalter, W. M. Jordan, Wm. Hildreth, B. F. Cavins, E. H. Swem, W. B. Riley, O. T. Conger, D. D., and the present pastor, I. B. Timberlake. Rev. Timberlake is a native of Richmond, Va.; graduating from Richmond college in 1885; later from the Theological seminary of Louisville, and beginning his ministry here in March 88, since which the church has been much revived. He is chaplain of First Ind. Reg. Natl. Guards.

Culbertson Ave. Baptist.—T. L. McNeece, a graduate of the Louisville Theological seminary, organized a mission Sabbath school in Ecker's hall in the summer of 88, and a few months later the school was held in Silver Grove. The next year, Rev. McNeece purchased a lot on Culbertson avenue, and erected the building now occupied. The church organization was effected in August 89, with some 20 members, the present number being about 50. Rev. McNeece was succeeded in August 91, by Rev. J. G. Barker, a native of Park Co., Ind.; educated in St. Louis, for 5 years in the ministry and still pursuing theological studies in the Louisville seminary. Ollie Owens the Vincennes street druggist, has charge of the Sunday school.

Protestant Episcopal.—The organization of St. Paul's P. E. church was effected July 18, 34. A frame building was erected on Spring street, near E. 3rd, in 1837, at a cost of about $5,000. This served until the present building on Main street above Sixth, was erected in 64-5, and which cost about $15,000. The membership is now 180, and a lot has been purchased at the corner of 11th and Market sts, where a $20,000 edifice will be erected shortly. The names of the rectors have been Ashbel Steele, 37; J. C. Britton, 41; Edw. Lounsberry, 42: B. W. Hickox, 43; W. K. Saunders, 44; T. H. L. Laird, 47; J. B. Ramsdell, 49: John Martin, J. A. Childs, 50; J. M. Gorhom, 52; J. S. Wallace 59; E. J. Purdy 62; T. G. Cower, 65; David Pise, 68; John Gierlow, 77; F. B. Dunham, 78; Walter Scott, 81; C. C. Lemon, 87; F. J. Mallett, 88, and A. B Nicholas, who came Oct. 15, 89. Rev. Nicholas was born in Manchester, Eng., removing to Ohio, in boyhood. He graduated from Kenyon college 71, serving as rector at Sandusky, O., and as general missionary prior to accepting the New Albany charge.

Park Christian.—Alexander Campbell taught that the bible alone should be relied upon as the rule of faith, without the aid of man-made creeds, and upon this foundation the nucleus of the Christian church, as now known, was organized by Campbell and his followers about 1826. The Park Christian church was founded May 19, 1835, by 43 persons who had withdrawn from the Baptist church. Thos. J. Murdock was licensed to preach, and D. G. Stewart was minister for a time, when T. Vaughn succeeded. J. E. Noyes, Jas. Slider, J. J. Moss, J. M. Mathes, Jas. Jamison, Geo. P. Adams, J. M. Henry, W. F. Parker, and J. J. Parsons, were ministers prior to the formation of the Central church. Succeeding these we find the names of J. W. Sewell, J. H. Hamilton, N. R. Dale, F. N. Calvin, M. N. Reed, J. B. Gibson, Geo. P. Simmons, M. Pitman, Prof. Reese, W. H. Applegate, and Rev. O. E. Palmer, the present pastor. Rev. Palmer is a native of Port Washington, Ohio, educated at Bethany college, and served as pastor at Lafayette this state, before coming to the Park church, 1888. A brick building was erected in 1836, which with lot cost about $6,000. This was torn down in 68, and the present commodious edifice erected the following year. The value of the Park church property is about $15,000, and present membership not far from 200.

Central Christian.—This society was organized in January 72, with 30 members, and the church building on Spring, near E. Fifth, was erected the following summer. Rev. J. L. Parsons, remained with the church about five years from its organization; was succeeded by J. C. Tully, 77; H. K. Pendleton, 82; L. H. Stein, 85; J. H. Crutcher, 90; H. T. Wilson, 91, and T. R. Bridges, who came in February of the present year. Rev. Bridges is a native of Ghent, Carroll county, Ky.; graduated from the Hanover (Ind.) college in 87; taught Latin and Greek at New Castle, Ky., for a year; graduated in theology from the Kentucky University; and the New York Theological seminary, after which he took a tour in Europe, and has now settled down to the ministry in New Albany. The present membership of the Central church is over 490. J. L. Stacy is Superintendent of the Sabbath school which has a large attendance.

<h2 style="text-align:center">ROMAN CATHOLIC CHURCHES.</h2>

Holy Trinity.—A pontifical succession in the Roman Catholic church has been clearly traced backwards through the history of the early church fathers to the honorable chair of St. Peter. So it appears that this church is able to establish a longer continuous claim than any other organization among christian nations. The first R. C. congregation in New Albany was the Holy Trinity, organized by the Rev. Louis Neyron in 1836. A frame church was built next year and Father Neyron also attended the congregation on the "Knobs" alternate Sundays until 1851, when the brick church was erected. after which he spent all his time here. Father Neyron died at Notre Dame, Jan. 7, 88, in his 98th year, Holy Trinity having paid him a 500 annuity for over 20 years. L. Gueguen succeeded in 64, and John Mougin in the same year, assisted part of the time by Revs. Ginnsz and Fleischman until 1881, when Rev. J. B. Kelly was appointed. Father Kelly is an Irishman, in America since 63, completing his studies in philosophy and theology at Montreal, Canada, and serving as pastor at Cambridge, Ind., prior to accepting his charge in New Albany. The Holy Trinity school was erected in 1882 by Father Kelly, and the superintendence of the handsome home for the Sisters of Providence came next. Much expense has also been put upon the church and cemetery. Father Kelly is assisted by Rev. J. F. Stanton of Richmond, Ind., who graduated from Sulpitian Seminary, Baltimore, Md., and has been assistant here since July, 90. Over 350 children are in regular attendance at the parochial school, in charge of 8 Sisters of Providence, Prof. B. W. B. Kingston having charge of the advanced male department, and 400 families are adherents to this church. The church and school property is valued at $100,000.

St. Marys Congregation.—-This society also known as the church of the Annunciation, dates its organization back to 1853, when Father A. Munschina gathered the German Catholics together, and secured the old house of the Holy Trinity church. Father Weutz came in 54, and was succeeded in 57 by the present Very Rev. Dean Faller. The following year the present handsome brick church edifice, corner Spring and E. 8th sts was erected at a cost of $20,000, all paid by the pastor's vigorous work. Rev. C. Doebbener who came in 67, five years later erected St. Marys Academy, a five-story brick structure, at a cost of $29,000. This is owned by the Sisters of St. Francis, who conduct a parish school, having under their charge 360 pupils, which includes the boys school of St. Joseph's hall. This building was erected by the Rev. F. I. Klein who came 1872, and who died from a fall which he received June 4, 86, while superintending work on the church. Rev. Faller returned to this charge July 14, 86, donated $13,000 to complete the improvements and in 88 built the handsome rectorage at a cost of $7,500. The seating capacity of the church is over 1,000 and the entire church property is worth over $100,000. There are over 450 families in the congregation. Prof. M. Merl has charge of the high class for boys, presiding over the church organ as well. Rev. Faller was born in Alsace, Germany, Jan. 3, 1824, and landed at Vincennes May 1, 1840 where after a six years course in the dio-

cesan seminary, he was ordained to the ministry in 46. Having since inherited a
goodly sum, he has contributed to church enterprises over $50,000 from his personal
funds. Rev. Frank A. Roell is a native of, and was educated at, Oldenburg, Ind.,
completing his studies at St. Meinards Seminary, 1878, and after ordination his first
charge was at St. Marks church in Perry county. Father Roell came to New Albany
Jan. 80, and has since been assisting Father Faller at St. Mary's church.

German Evangelical.—This church organization was effected in New Albany,
Oct. 25, 1837, with 43 members, of whom only one, Mrs. Armstrong, formerly Mrs.
Meyer, is now living. Rev. Henry Evers continued as pastor for several years.
Meetings were held in the school house and old court house until 1843, when a church
was built on State street near Oak. Rev. Fr. Dulitz, who died in Cincinnati, Jan.
92, at the advanced age of 95 years, was pastor from 43 to 47. Rev. Meyer served
the church for seven years from 53, during which the organization was greatly
strengthened. Revs. Abele, Riedel, Brandau and Daubert served the society prior
to the present pastor. In 1865, the Zion Lutheran congregation consolidated with
the above, and Sept. 4, 1870, the present handsome house of worship was erected,
which with lot cost over $20,000. The interior of the church was burned in June 86,
but was rebuilt as good as before. The organization represents 150 families and is in
charge of Rev. G. Dietz, who came to this pastorate Feb. 79. He is a native of Germany, educated at Basle, Switzerland, and has been in America since 1864.

Colored Churches.—Crosby chapel and Jones chapel are African M. E. churches, and are well patronized by the negroes of New Albany. The Second Baptist
church is also for colored people, and has a substantial brick church formerly occupied by the Presbyterians. Value of the church property belonging to the colored
churches is about $20,000.

New Albany Y. M. C. A.—George Williams was the leading spirit in organ-

izing the Young Men's
Christian Association in
London, in 1844. For 20
years there was no special
uniform'ty in conducting
the different societies; but
about that time the work
was more clearly outlined,
and has been endorsed by
all evangelical churches as
an auxiliary to christian
work. It has made a won-
derful development and
the remarkable progress of
the physical culture department reflects credit upon
the zealous workers for
sanitary reform. In city
life the gymnasium is an
essential feature for grow-
ing young men, and we are glad to note that New Albany is to have a well fitted

building as the permanent home of the Y. M. C. A. The structure with lot will cost over $30,000, the principal part of which has already been subscribed, and the building is now well under way. It will front 60 feet on Main and 110 feet on Pearl, and the basement will contain a complete gymnasium, swimming pool, lavatories, etc.

J. F. Gebhart, the president of the Y. M. C. A., is superintendent of the woolen mills, under which heading he will be mentioned; W. C. Nunemacher, treasurer, is noticed elsewhere, and E. H. Jones, general secretary, is a native of Allegheny City, reared in Cleveland, graduated from the high school of that city, for several years was a watch maker, and six years ago entered the Association work, coming to New Albany Jan. 15, 1890, since when his zeal in the cause has made many friends for him in this city.   **1312125**

Main Street S. S. Mission.—This philanthropy was commenced by A. W. Bentley in 1861, as a refugee Sunday school, and the interest which secured a permanent hold on the people in that vicinity continues to the present. Jno. F. Gebhart became superintendent in 1869, and has been zealously engaged in the charge ever since. Some 325 names are enrolled with an average attendance of 250 children each Sabbath day.

EDUCATIONAL INTERESTS.—With an intelligent populace, the educational interests of a city, has much to do with its desirability as a place for residence, and New Albany stands in the front rank in this particular. The founders of the village were zealous promoters of education, and a permanent endowment fund of $5,000 was set apart, the interest of which was to go perpetually for school improvements. In the first year of development here, a large log school house was erected at the corner of State and Spring. This was also used as a place for religious worship for two or three years. Stephen Beers was the first school teacher of whom we have record. Mr Corcelius taught a select school in the upper part of Jas. Anderson's shoe shop about 1820. An act incorporating the New Albany school was passed Jan. 8, 21, which placed the control in a board of managers and John A. Spaulding continued as sole teacher for many years. In 38 the school was divided into male and female departments and additional teachers hired. As the accumulation of the interest on the endowment fund amounted to a considerable sum, it was determined to erect a building on W. First street, corner Spring; and the neat two story brick known as Scribner's High school for boys, was completed in the spring of 1849. In 1853, the city assumed control of the public schools, under a board of trustees, and a complete system of grading was arranged. The New Albany High school was opened in Oct. 53, with George H. Harrison in charge. The enrollment of July, 54, shows 1,570 pupils, with 28 teachers in service, but the law to provide for a general and uniform system of common schools, having that fall been declared unconstitutional, school progress was practically closed for a year or two. Charles Burnes was elected city superintendent and principal of the high school in 55; Jas. G. May, 57, and Geo. P. Brown, 64. The schools had been badly disarranged during the war, several of the buildings having been occupied as soldiers' hospitals, and Mr. Brown resigned his superintendency in 65. The schools were without a general superintendent for 8 years following, during which time a large number of private schools flourished. As late as 1870 only 28 per cent. of the school enumeration attended the free schools. In that year the Female High school was organized, and new life infused into the educational interests. Each succeeding year has added to the efficiency of the school system and to-day all classes of our citizens enjoy its privileges.

In addition to the usual funds received for free schools, the annual interest of the investment fund has been a great aid, and without the levy of excessive taxes, New Albany has kept abreast of the times in the free education of her youth. There are 12 substantial brick buildings ranging from 2 to 10 rooms each, 5 of these being used for the grammar grades. The new 8 room building now in course of constructon, corner Vincennes and Shelby streets, will cost when completed about $30,000, and be one of the handsomest public school structures in this section of Indiana. This will make the aggregate value of free school property in New Albany above $200,000, all clear from debt. The enumeration for 1891 was 7,854, and total enrollment 3,304 pupils, under charge of 64 teachers. The expense for salary was $29,378.75, and incidentals $6,872. The school taxables of New Albany aggregate $10,578,485.

In 1873 H. B. Jacobs was selected as Superintendent, continuing 9 years. Chas. F. Coffin served from 82 until the present incumbent was chosen in 85. Prof. J. B. Starr is a native of Byrnville, Harrison Co., was educated at Hartsville University, and has been teaching in Floyd county continuously for more than a quarter of a century. He served as principal of the Spring street grammar school for 7 years prior to having been promoted to the superintendency, thereby gaining an accurate knowledge of the school needs in the city, and preparing himself for the good work which he has accomplished in the general direction of the free schools.

The High School, corner Spring and Bank streets, is in charge of Prof. J. P. Funk, a native of Harrison Co., Ind., educated in the Indiana University, and later taking the A. M. degree from the Natl. Normal University of Lebanon, Ohio. He has been in school work for a quarter of a century, and principal here for 5 years past. The assistants are Mrs. Maggie Shrader and Miss Fannie Fawcett.

West Spring Street.—This school, located near W. 5th street, is a ten room building. Prof. J. M. Boyd, prin., is a native of Davies Co., educated in Fort Wayne College, and the National Normal University of Lebanon, Ohio. He has been in school work for 15 years, and in New Albany since 1887. His assistants are Lydia Towsend, Hattie E. Beeler, Lizzie Boss, Mattie Heth, Emma Pfrimmer, Philura Riley, Daisy Shaw, Emma Hannah and Hettie Stoy.

Main Street.—This school, located on E. Main, near 8th st., is in charge of Prof. W. S. McClure, a Pennsylvanian, educated in Normal Schools and at the Pittsburg Iron City Business College. He commenced teaching in 1868, and has been here since 74. His assistants are Annie E. Fowler, Cora Martin, Jennie Day, Mamie Beers, Nannie Magness, Belle Smith and Nettie Clark.

East Spring Street.—Prof. Geo. B. Haggett, principal of this school, is an Ohioan and received the degree of B. S. from Grand River Institute, in his native state, 1875, since which he has been in school work, having come to New Albany two years ago. He is assisted by Hattie Deeble, Belle Tombs, Lucy Barlow, Mary Mitchell, Lena Lonnon, Lillie Wheeler and Jennie Pennington.

Eleventh & Sycamore.—This building was erected in 1889, at a cost of $25,000. S. Ella Jones, principal, is a native of New Albany, and graduated from the High School. She is assisted by Eva Mathena, Marie Robellaz, Bettie Meek, Hester Patton, Millie Thomas, Jennie Riches and Florence Boardman.

Fourth near Spring.—Prof. Wm. Rady, principal is a native of this county, and after the common schools attended Hartsville University. He has been in school work since 1864, serving as principal of the Galvin school for 7 years prior to coming here in 1888. He is assisted by Nannie M. Beeler, Jennie Boyd, Carrie Hanmore, Annie McGarth, Lottie Ziegelbauer and Carrie Robertson.

West Union.—Prof. E. B. Walker, principal here for 2 years past, is a native of Washington Co., Ind., attended the DePauw and N. A. Commercial College. Mr. Walker has conducted normal schools in New Philadelphia and at our High School, and has served as teacher in the night session of the N. A. B. C. He is assisted by Augusta McKay, Emma Riley and Rosa Kent.

West Market.—Prof. G. A. Briscoe, prin., is a native of Greenville, educated at Danville & Valpariso, has been engaged in teaching for four years. He has recently taken the place of Miss Sue Hooper, who had been teaching here for the past 25 years. He is assisted by Jennie Elzy, Hattie Sands and Kate C. Huckeby.

German School.—Prof. J. B. James is a native of France, after an education in the county schools he commenced teaching and studying until he now carries a state license, and has been in the school work for the past 30 years. He is assisted by Clara Gohman, Lizzie Meyers and Lizzie Bohl.

Colored Schools.—The advanced colored pupils are under charge of Prof. W. O. Vance, at Scribner high school building on First and Spring. He is assisted by Mrs. D. S. Vance and Jessie Clay. Schools are also kept at West Second, D. S. Maxwell, prin., assisted by Ella Rickman, and on Division street with C. A. Martin, prin., assisted by Susie Banks.

The School Board are M. A. Weir, who has been president for a dozen years; J. G. Harrison, secretary, and P. R. Stoy, treasurer; all prominently connected in business and thoroughly awake to the cause of education. The principals and teachers have been selected and promoted upon merit, and it is doubtful if any city in the Union of this size can be found having a better system of public schools, more convenient buildings and general accommodations for the children—and what is best of all no bonded or floating debt.

DePAUW COLLEGE.
A GENEROUSLY ENDOWED NEW ALBANY INSTITUTE.

Through the bequests of the Hon. W. C. DePauw, this historic place for education will soon receive a liberal endowment that will insure its prompt enlargement and continuous prosperity. Its successful progress will be regarded with much favor by all good citizens of New Albany, and will reflect honor upon its generous endower.

The central portion of the college building, was erected in 1852, as a boarding school for young ladies, under the name of Indiana Asbury Female College. In 1866 the building was sold to satisfy a mortgage and transferred to other owners; but the same year enterprising Methodists decided to celebrate their century of work in America, by a repurchase of this institute, which through the liberal donations of Mr. DePauw and other citizens of this city was accomplished, and the building presented to the Indiana Conference free from debt. It was opened in Sept. 66, by Rev. Erastus Rowley, D. D., and commenced a prosperous career. The students increased so rapidly that additional room was required and the ever generous Mr. DePauw erected the east wing of the building at a cost of about $10,000. The building was partially burned in 1880, but rebuilt better than before. It is a three story brick structure, which can furnish recitation room for about 500 pupils. Up to 1889 the college had been chiefly devoted to the education of young women. when it was decided to establish a high grade academic course for both sexes. That this decision was wise has been clearly demonstrated by its increased prosperity. DePauw College, although conducted under auspices of the M. E. Conference is not sectarian in its teachings, requiring only a high moral standard of action for admission to its benefits. The curriculum covers astronomy, chemistry, English, French, German, Greek and Latin languages, history and art, mathematics, philosophy, physics, physiology and special studies in elocution.

The library contains more than a thousand volumes, and the labaratory and apparatus are quite complete, although it will soon receive large additions and improvements. The bequest of the late W. C. DePauw gives $1,000 a year for betterments each year until the settlement of the estate, when it is to be endowed by 5 per cent. of the residue of this estate estimated at from three to five millions of dollars, which will enable the institute to add every needed improvement and greatly enlarge its sphere of action, making a school of learning of which New Albany may well feel a just pride.

The May Brothers, Jas. W. and Benoni A., Principals, came from a family of teachers and have inherited the disposition and faculty so necessary for complete success in that line. James G. May, grandfather of the above, was one of the best known educators in southern Indiana, having been a teacher for 60 years, and early connected with the New Albany schools. Their father, William W. May, formerly principal of the Male Academy, taught in New Albany for fourteen years. The May Brothers were educated at Syracuse University, and taught in the Academy at Salem for several years prior to taking charge of DePauw College in 1889. They are zealous workers and are meeting with a justly merited success.

The Conservatory of Music, under charge of Miss Addie Packard has gained a wide notoriety for its efficiency in both vocal and instrumental music. In all departments diplomas or degrees are conferred upon those entitled to the same, and the Conservatory is becoming very popular. Miss Packard is assisted by J. F. Surman, teacher of violin, and Mrs. C. Carr, teacher of vocal culture, and the College, in all its departments, will be kept abreast of the times, so that not only New Albany citizens, but those from distant cities and states will accept its superior advantages.

NEW ALBANY BUSINESS COLLEGE.
CORNER STATE AND MARKET STREETS.

Practical business education has grown in popular favor very rapidly within the last quarter century,, and good business colleges are now so numerous and well conducted that young people, of either sex, can readily avail themselves of these privileges. In fact at the present time a young lady or gentleman can scarcely afford to enter upon the active duties of life without first having obtained a practical business education,   .

What is now known as the New Albany Business College, was established by Wm. Purdy in the Woodward Hall, Lower First and Main streets, with James McMannus as penman, September 2d, 1865. This school was then known as Purdy's Business College. About five years later Marquam & Johnson purchased Mr. Purdy's school and then named it The New Albany Business College. Marquam and Johnson had a branch school at Louisville, and another at Lexington, Ky. It was at the latter that I. G. Strunk was a student and teacher, and after graduating Aug. 20, 1872, was employed to come to New Albany to teach in this College. He was duly installed as principal Sept. 2, 1872; on the first of November following purchased a half interest, and on the 18th of the same month became sole proprietor. The College then occupied one room about 18x30 feet on the third floor of the Vernia Block, Spring and Pearl street. Here bright new furniture was purchased, which at that time was considered the finest around the Falls. The seating capacity was soon found to be too small and another room the same size was added. Still the space was found to be inadequate, when in 1876, the school was removed to the old spiritual hall, Cannon Block, Pearl st. On May 15, 1877, Prof. D. M. Hammond was admitted as a partner when the firm name became Strunk & Hammond. Dec. 1, 1882, the seating capacity was found too small and the school was removed to Maennerchor Halle, corner State and Market streets. At that time this was thought to be too large for the business, but three months later it became necessary to teach four sessions a day, in order to accommodate the applicants for admission. Prof. Strunk, in May, 1885, retired on account of failing health but a year later reentered the College- At that time Prof. Hammond assumed the position of president, and I. G- Strunk as secretary, since which no firm name has been used.

Tha College has prospered until it now occupies the second and third floor of the large Sloan block, Market and State street, having two distict Departments, viz: the Commercial and the Shorthand and Typewriting department. In the former are taught bookkeeping, penmanship, arithmetic, spelling, commercial, law, correspondence and business practice. In the latter are taught shorthand, typewriting, penmanship, spelling, correspondence and false syntax. Miss J. Annie Jones, is principal, of the shorthand department, and Miss Fannie Forse has charge of the typewriting division. The New Albany Business College, as now established, presents superior facilities, and prepares its graduates to fill important and responsible positions with success in the various directions of business life. That it has been successfully continued for nearly 29 years, is a credit to our city, and its proprietors are meeting with an encouragement which is the due reward of efficiency and good business tact.

American Express.—The business of carying small packages was begun in 1840, by W. F. Harnden and spread in its development to the express trade, which now has for its motto, "speed and safety," receiving packages of any reasonable size or weight. The American Express commenced business about the middle of the present century and has ever kept abreast of the times, adding new lines and offices as fast as the contingencies of the case demands, until it now has 6,000 offices and covers some 45,000 miles of railroad and steamship lines. The money orders of this company are convenient, cheap and safe, while its commission purchase system is very popular with those who have investigated. The American Express was run jointly with the Adams, at this place, until about 12 years ago, since which the business has rapidly grown.

During the season for strawberries, raspberries and other small fruits, the express business is especially brisk, necessitating the use of several cars daily to cover these shipments. William B. Hinkley is a native of this place, served for 2 years in the employ of the Adams Express, and after a year as driver for the American took charge of this in 1887.

Adams Express.—The Adams Express Company was first organized to carry packages between New York and Buffalo about 1850, and has each year been adding new lines and offices, until it now has numerous agencies extending well over the

United States. Soon after its organization the company established an office in New Albany, which is now held at No. 124, Pearl street, and is transacting a large business at this place. In the fruit season, a specialty is made of shipping strawberries, raspberries and other fruits and vegetables, which go principally to Chicago and Indianapolis. J. N. Morris, agent, is a native of this county, and had been in the employ of the Adams Express Co. for the past two years as chief assistant, prior to his appointment upon the death of J. B. Morris, in March last.

U. S. Express Co.—The United States Express was organized about 1856, and has since been adding new lines and offices as fast as the contingencies of the case demanded. The company own express franchise, over 27,000 miles of railroad, and, through connection with the Pacific Express, ships goods direct to 10,000 agencies.

This company established an office in this city, in June, 88. L. Hammersmith has been in charge here since the office was located in New Albany, and is assisted by John Hahn, Jr., who is a native of this place. Mr. Hammersmith is also connected with the Louisville and New Albany transfer trade described in the following article:

Louisville & New Albany Freight Transfer.—Charles Hammersmith, deceased, commenced the freight transfer trade between this city and Louisville about 1860, and his son Louis grew up in the business. Upon the death of his father in 1875, L. Hammersmith succeeded to the management and from time to time has increased the teaming capacity until now some 40 men and above 50 horses are engaged in the trade. Spring vehicles are used for freights requiring careful handling, and heavy drays for more ponderous goods. In Nov., 1890, Jacob L. Young, who had been an assistant in the business for some time past, became a partner with Mr. Hammersmith in the transfer trade. The firm contracts for any kind of hauling, but especial attention is given for the transfer of goods between the jobbers, merchants and manufacturers of Louisville and New Albany, the teams making a regular daily round, for the delivery of special orders. Messrs. Hammersmith & Young are each expert horsemen and employ men of integrity and sobriety. They are supplied with all the necessary apparatus for handling ponderous machinery, and the steady increase in this trade assists in the promotion of the commercial relations between the two cities which it connects. Orders taken at U. S. Exp. office, 65 State street, or at the stable office on Elm street, near 14th. Louisville office at No. 153, Third street. Telephone connections at each office.

Slider's Transfer.—John T. Slider came to New Albany in childhood and for 30 years past has been in the transfer trade. His son, E. T. Slider, has grown up in the business. The twain occupy stables together, but have separate offices and each has a distinct trade. The Sliders keep a dozen teams or more and give employment to from 15 to 25 men transfering all kinds of light or heavy freight in this city, as well as between here and Louisville. Covered spring wagons are used for household goods and light merchandise, while heavy trucks and all necessary apparatus are provided for weighty and bulky articles. E. T. Slider is also proprietor of the line of sprinklers, which are a great convenience to our citizens as dust layers, in dry weather. Every kind of hauling receives prompt attention from the Messrs. Sliders. Morris M. Slider, a brother of the above, is general soliciting agent, and accompanies the transfer teams to Louisville, in each daily round, to see that all orders are properly filled. The stables and offices are on Elm street, below State. Louisville offices at Kessler, Koch & Co.'s, 509 W. Main street.

W. U. Telegraph.—This company was formed in 1856, by the consolidation of three companies, then doing business in the United States. The Western Union transacted business in New Albany soon after its first organization, starting off with less than 10,000 messages a year. and is now above 120,000. Geo. H. Godfrey, local manager, is a native of Genuesee Co., N. Y., and commenced with the Western Union in Michigan, in 1858, came to New Albany July 8, 61, has been in charge of the office here since, for the first 19 years doing all the work, but now is assisted by P. M. Mathers, of Bloomington, who has been here for 7 years, and P. C. Garrett, of this place, who has recently commenced here.

The W. U. Tel. Co. owns or controls nearly 200,000 miles of poles, having three times as great a length of wire, and over 10,000 offices. It annually transmits over 50 millions of messages, which are handled by about 22,000 operators, nearly half of whom are in railroad employ, in addition to handling W. U. Telegraph business.

The Ohio Valley Telephone Co.—The wonders of development in electrical science, within the past quarter of a century, have been amazing indeed, and among these, none have surpassed the telephone. If any scientist, 25 years since, had proclaimed that our generation would yet speak to each other, when miles of space intervened, he would at once have been taken for a crank, or a fit subject for an asylum, and yet space has now been practically annihilated, and we talk with friend or customer a hundred miles or more distant through the aid of a telephone wire, with ease, thereby greatly facilitating commercial transactions. In this busy age, when time is worth more than money, the conveniences and benefits derived through the use of the telephone are so numerous, that it is poor business policy for any progressive firm to be without the advantages to be gained by it. The mechanism of the telephone to the wants of commerce was first perfected March, 1876, and it spread with wonderful alacrity to all progressive cities. The Ohio Valley Telephone Co. extended their lines from Louisville to New Albany it 1882, but on account of arbitrary law in Indiana, reducing the price below a remunerative standard, the business was withdrawn in 85, and after the obnoxious law had been repealed, it was reestablished again in May, 89. There are now about 100 phones in use here, but at least three times that number of business firms would be greatly benefitted by its use and should be supplied. The more subscribers there are the more valuable the service becomes. Non-subscribers pay 15 cents for a call with Louisville, but New Albany subscribers get an 8 cent rate, making a considerable saving to those having much business with the metropolis across the river. The Ohio Valley Telephone Co. gives connection with 60 cities and towns in Ky. and Ind., within a radius of 100 miles from this place, toll rates being charged at usual prices. There are 2,500 phones in use in Louisville, the central office being at 444, Jefferson street. H. N. Gifford, general manager, has been with the company since 1879, and has built up an efficient and satisfactory service. The New Albany branch, since May, 89, has been in charge of Alice Frazee, as chief operator, with Kate Williams and Blake Frazee assistants for day and night.

Water Works.—Perhaps no other single agent, contributes more largely to the general prosperity of a manufacturing city, than first-class water works, and in this respect New Albany is highly favored. When the project was started in 1873, it did not meet with prompt encouragement from our capitalists; but John F. Gebhart and others who saw the immense advantages to be derived from a manufacturing standpoint, persisted in the undertaking and the articles of association were filed Dec. 5th, 1874, by J. F. Gebhart, W. S. Culbertson, Jesse J. Brown, Morris McDonald, J. K. Woodward, Sr., R. G. McCord, D. C. Hill and H. O. Cannon. The $100,000 capital stock not all having been taken, W. H. Dillingham was shortly afterwards induced to subscribe, and notwithstanding the fact that it was many years before a dividend had been declared, he continued to be a liberal encourager of the enterprise, purchasing stock from time to time until he now owns more than one-fourth of the present $233,000 capital. Active work commenced in 1875, and the plant was opened for use in July of the Centenial year. Mr. Gebhart, having been chosen president, W. N. Mahon, secretary, and Frank Shefold, superintendent, at the start.

The mains have been extended, reservoir capacity enlarged, and improvements added from time to time, until the works are now first-class in every respect, and represent an investment of over $365,000. The pumping station on the river bank, at the foot of W. Eighth street, is equipped with a battery of boilers and two pumping engines. One of these has a capacity of raising $1\frac{1}{2}$ millions of gallons daily, and the other $2\frac{1}{4}$ millions, the running of the works consuming 5 tons of coal daily. The daily consumption of water averages about a million gallons daily, which is but little more than one-fourth the capacity of the plant. The intake or suction pipe extends from the pump house 200 feet, with its mouth covered by a strainer, in deep water, 30 feet from the beach, at low water mark. The reservoirs are located on Silver Hills, about a mile distant, by air line, from the pumping house, and at an elevation of over 200 feet above the average plateau of the city. Three old reservoirs have a holding capacity of ten million gallons. The new reservoir, built in 1891, cover 4 acres, is 18 feet in depth, and has a capacity of about twenty million gallons, so that a supply sufficient for nearly 4 weeks can be held in the reserve. The water is floated slowly, through opposite diagonal corners, from one reservoir to the other, until delivered into the new one, allowing sufficient chance for settling and aeration by exposure to the strong current of air on the knobs.

At the first test, July, 1876, 8 leads of hose, with inch nozzles, were attached to the hydrants, on State street, and simultaneous streams thrown 125 feet high. There are 166 fire plugs. The original contract with the city required 11 fire-hydrants to each mile, and as there are 20 miles of mains, there properly should be 54 more hydrants, which rightly placed would avoid the necessity for long stretching of the hose. The pressure is so even and abundant, and the fire service so efficient, that disastrous fires seldom occur, and insurance risks are written at about half what they were prior to the building of these works, so that the saving in premiums alone is much greater to the citizens of New Albany than the entire cost of water rental to the city. The first 100 fire-hydrants are charged at $100 each, the next 100 at $75 each, and all above 200 at $60 each. A large amount of the present prosperity of this city is due to the efficiency of these works and the very low rate given by the company to factories and others who use water in large quantities. The rate made is $12\frac{1}{2}$ cents per 1000 gallons where the daily average is a single thousand, and this is graded in proportionate quantities, running as low as 5 cents. Not only is the metre rate low, but the prices for domestic use, when compared with 60 other cities throughout the Union, is found to be about half as much as the usual charge. Many kinds of diseases are attributable to foul air and polluted water, but diptheria, typhoid fever and kindred complaints, are found in country villages, where only well water is used. When they become epidemic in cities, they are sometimes supposed to have been caused by river water, while perhaps more justly attributable to other sources. Drainage from cesspools and penetration by common sewage, often pollute wells at a greater distance than would naturally be expected. Well or cistern water when kept covered and stagnant become a more fruitful field in which to multiply bachteria or other noxious germs than. flowing water. The rapid and continuous churning which the river water gets in coming over the Falls, results in thorough aeration, and in our judgment, the New Albany Water Works supply is far safer for general use than any of the products of the city wells. Careful analysis has been made by 2 chemists of note, and the amount of organic matter found in a gallon of water, taken from the hydrant last fall when the river was lower than it had been for ten (10) years, was found to be infinitesimally small. The chemical tests showed the water to be "pure, wholesome and fit for domestic use."

The net earnings of the water works for 1871 were 7½ per cent., which, for a concern requiring constant additions and replacements, is small. The pumping station is in charge of C. H. Fitch, a native of Mass., who came to New Albany in 1845. After learning the machinist's trade he served as engineer on a steamboat for many years, and has been chief engineer of these works ever since their erection. As before stated, Wm. H. Dillingham became a stockholder in the enterprise about 1875, and his interests in the same has continued to increase from time to time. At a sacrifice to his business interests in Louisville, he accepted the presidency of this company at its last election. He is a native of Mass., and has been a resident of Louisville since March 1st, 1847. E. J. Brooks, secretary and treasurer. is a native of Maine, came to New Albany in 1855, and has been connected with the various interests of the city since that time, excepting a couple of years that he was interested in the railroad at Madison, Ind. Fred. Rapp, superintendent, has been connected with the company since its organization. The directors, elected in Jan., 1891, were W. H. Dillingham, J. K. Woodward, Sr., John Shrader, Sr., Chas. Sackett, G. C. Cannon, E. J. Brooks and the Hon. G. V. Howk, who died a few days after his election. The magnitude and successful management of the Water Works is a very important feature in our manufacturing development, presenting great inducements in pure water at lower rates than elsewhere; with superior protection against fire, resulting in low cost of insurance. The enterprise is deserving of business encouragement from every owner of real estate.

Light, Heat & Power Co.—A company was organized Jan. 91, for the production of light, heat and power by electricity. The works were purchased July of last year by the present well known proprietors. Since which time extensive improvements have been added and the plant is now a very complete and well equipped electrical concern. The inventions of the present century are very numerous, but in no other direction has so many wonderful results been developed as through electrical science. The census reports of 1880, had but a brief mention of electrical progression, while those of 1890, show many millions of dollars invested in the manufacture of various electrical appliances. and many thousands of people employed in this direction. Perhaps the developments in electric light and electric power have increased more rapidly within the last decade than any other branch of science. Fifteen years ago—mere toys—in an experimental stage, these have now become the necessities of the age, and no progressive city can afford to be without them. Marcus Ruthenburg, superintendent of the above plant, engaged in the study of solving electrical problems pertaining to mechanism in 1880, has kept abreast of the times in electrical development, and the new plant has been fitted up with special reference to having it as nearly perfect, in all departments as it is practical to make it. The works are located on the river bank at E. Ninth and Water streets and cost about $100,000. With a battery of four boilers, 6x16 feet, of Stearn's manufacture, Erie, Pa, creating an aggregate of 600 horse power; and two magnificent engines of 300 horse power, each of Armington & Sims make, sufficient electrical power can be generated to run a number of factories, in addition to the Highland Electric Railroad, and the necessities for electric light. The line has 50 miles of wire in use here, extending from Silver Grove to Silver Hills, and ramifying throughout the city. The machinery is planted on solidly constructed stone foundations, above the highwater mark of 1884 flood. The output of the 60 arc-light machine having all been taken, another dynamo of like production has recently been added to supply the increasing demand. Three National incandescent machines, of Euclaire, Wis.. manufactories. have combined capacity of 3,000 lights, are being largely patronized on account of the superior illuminating power. Altogether this enterprise is meeting with a well merited success, and is fully demonstrating the efficiency of the management. John S. Briggs, president, is a native of Floyd county; a resident of New Albany from boyhood, and in the hardware trade prior to engaging in this enterprise. August Barth, secretary and treasurer, is owner of an extensive tannery, under which heading he will have mention, while Otto Hoffman, vice president, is a coal dealer, and will be mentioned in that department.

Gas Light & Coke Co.—This company was organized in 1854, to supply illuminating gas for New Albany. The location of the works is at the corner of Sycamore and E. 4th streets, on a lot 130x190 feet, more than half of which is covered by fine brick buildings. The Gasometre is corner of Bank and Sycamore, holding 60,000 cubic feet. A new reservoir will be built, in the near future, to hold 350,000 feet When the present management commenced a dozen years ago the price of gas was $3.00. This has been reduced one-half and extensive improvements added to the plant. Notwithstanding the fact of electric plants and lights, the consumption of gas has steadily increased. The price charged for illuminating gas is $1.50 per 1,000 feet, and for fuel purposes $1.00 per 1,000. Some 600 customers and about 600 street lamps are supplied.

In 1888 a 50 light arc dynamo was put in and with the increasing demand, another of like capacity was added in the latter part of 1889. A 1,000 light incandescent Thomson Houston machine was put in, from which a steady and satisfactory light is given The electric plant is equipped with a battery of boilers and two large engines, and the combined consumption of coal, for gas and electric light purposes, is 5,000 tons annually. The plant is under the superintendence of J. W. Dunbar. a native of this city, and a graduate of the Scribner High school, who has been connected with these works for 10 years past, and is thoroughly acquainted with every minutiae of operation.

W. S. Culbertson, the president of this organization, is the well known president of the First National Bank,. J. K. Woodward, Jr., the secretary and treasurer, was born and reared in this city, graduated from Harvard college, and has been with this company since 1880. In the various operations of the company some 25 hands are employed.

G. H. Devol, vice president, is in the stove and tinware trade, where he will receive
nention. Jas. O. English, cashier, has been with the company for a dozen years.
. K. Woodward, Sr., in the mercantile trade, is also on the board of directors, in ad-
lition to the psesident, vice president, secretary and superintendent.

MANUFACTURING INDUSTRIES.

In observing the many advantages of this favored section of our state, it is a matter
f wonder to the careful observer that there are not more general manufactories in
Iew Albany.   To be sure we have an encouraging number, but in this pamphlet we
ope to sufficiently demonstrate, that, taking all in all, there are few better localities
1 the wide world for manufacturing than this location at the foot of the Falls.
Vhile the mercantile interests of a community are an essential feature and the
rofessional talent a necessary part of a city, it is generally admitted that thriving
ianufacturing industries are the great *desideratum*, giving greater permenancy and
apidity of growth than all other interests combined.   The merchant brings to us the
ommodities of commerce and is usually generous in dividing his profits to enterprises
f public good; but the successful manufacturer opens a permanent investment for
apital at remunerative rates, gives employment to the laborers of a community and
nhances the value of all farm products in his immediate section by providing a
ome market.   New Albany with her superior river and railroad facilities, well
roven healthfulness and picturesque surroundings, offers superior inducements to
hose who may desire to make investments within her borders.   Lands are cheap,
iborers plenty; educational, social and religious advantages of high grade; her
itizens are noted for their culture, hospitality and generous welcome toward good
eople from other states and countries.   With a map before him, any observer may
eadily see how centrally and advantageously this city is located, with reference to
oal, iron and lumber interests, and the facilities to reach the principal markets.
Ianufacturers, capitalists, or those in search of healthful homes, after well weighing
ur surroundings, cannot fail to ascertain the great advantages possessed by New
.lbany.   Many who in the emigration excitement of the past decade, sought for
omes in the west and south, have realized their mistake, and have returned to this
icinity.   New Albany township will in time become densely populated, and the
urrounding acres of this city can furnish abundance of room upon which to build a
ity of 500,000 inhabitants.   This is already a city of homes, in which a large
ercentage of heads of families own commodious residences, with plenty of breathing
pace.   With Silver Grove, Silver Hills and other desirable plats, which will be
ientioned under real estate matters, there can be no difficulty in procuring reasonably
heap and favorable locations for coming development.

But we have digressed—manufacturing is our theme.   As industrial establishments,
se the raw material of the country, thereby bringing remunerative prices to the
wner and producer of such articles, and dispense large amounts in weekly wages,
rhich revert to the tills of our merchants and mechanics, the municipality can well
fford to give them liberal encouragement.   On thriving manufacturing concerns
he growth and continuing prosperity of our city largely depends, and those who are
ssisting industrial enterprises by their capital or brains, should receive due credit.
n succeeding pages we shall give a separate mention of our principal manufactories,
et forth the features which have contributed to their upbuilding, and have a word

to say regarding their originators and present proprietors, devoid however of t
usual fulsome praise and unworthy personal laudation, which generally characteri:
descriptive writings.

DePAUW PLATE GLASS COMPANY.

POLISHED AND ROUGH PLATE GLASS.

In reviewing the various industries of this place, with a view ot conveying to t
outside world a knowledge of its resources, we desire to identify the greater acco
plishments, with those whose energy and enterprise have been mainly instrumen
in our manufacturing success. The DePauw Works have gained such marked succ
in the magnitude of their operations, and the wide spread distribution of their war
as to justly entitle this plant to first consideration. It is the giant industrial ent,
prise of this section of country, and the most complete of its kind in the Uni,
States.

The history of plate glass in America, up to 1872, was one of continuous rever
and bankruptcy. Previous to that time several attempts had been made, but e;
had met with final disaster. In that year the late Hon. W. C. DePauw, of N
Albany, took the matter in hand with pluck and determination to succeed at wl,
ever cost. His business tact, abundant pecuniary resources and stamina brou;;
ultimate success; but it is stated that his actual losses from 1872 to 80, in cop·
with European rivals, was $600,000. It was a costly triumph, but nevertheless
to be proud of, and which has so soon revolutionized the plate glass trade of the wo:
reduced the price from 50 to 70 per cent. and permanently established under the s1,
and stripes, the successful manufacture of an indispensable commodity, which t
friend and foe predicted unfeasible.

The DePauw Plate Glass Co. cost in its establishment, including foundry, macl
shops and other necessary adjuncts, for the complete equipment, the gigantic sun
nearly $2,000,000. The plant is situated on a 30 acre tract of valuable ground, 1
the center of this city, between the Pennsylvania railroads and the river, traversed v
numerous side tracks, and having convenient boat landings for the line of stear
and barges owned by this company. The leading specialty of the works is, of cou
high grade plate glass, which has acquired a National reputation, and is produce
all sizes up to 150x200 inches, of finish and transparency equal to the best Fre
plate. Regarding the various buildings and machinery required to successf
operate this immense plant we have not space to attempt a detail. It suffices to
that the New Albany works has a capacity of 96 pots; Alexandria, Ind., 64·
Louisville, 35, a total of 192 pots for plate glass only. An extensive warehous
well filled with the finished product which is cut into sizes to meet all the ordi;
requirements of the trade while special orders are produced promptly.

Newland T. DePauw, president, is a native of Indiana, educated at DePauw 1
versity, and has been engaged in New Albany manufacturing for a dozen years ;
He is president of the Merchants National Bank and several prominent indus
concerns as will be seen under their respective headings. C. T. Doxey; vice p,
dent, is a leading business man of Anderson, Ind., who became a heavy stockhc
in these works in 1891. W. D. Keyes, secretary and treasurer, is a native of W
ington Co., Ind., and has been prominently identified with this plant for more ·.
20 years. John F. Merker, an enterprising New Albanian has recently been prom:
to the superintendency of this department.

W. C. DePAUW COMPANY.

WINDOW GLASS AND FRUIT JAR DEPARTMENT.

Although largely under the same management as the above, this is a distinct organization, known as the W. C. DePauw Co., the special branch of manufacture being single and double strength window glass and fruit jars. In this department there are more than a dozen buildings ranging in size from 20x80 feet to 80x130 all roughly fitted for their special requirements. Window glass is produced in all the required weights and sizes up to 50x76 inches, the annual shipments aggregating about 200,000 boxes.

The fruit jar department last year turned out 36,000 gross, which were shipped to jobbers in all sections of the country. An immense warehouse is kept filled with the various sizes, all carefully packed and marked ready for shipment at an hours notice. A complete box factory, in which millions of feet of lumber are annually consumed, kept in continuous operation. A complete system of water works and coal hoisting apparatus extends from the river's edge to all departments of the works and every requirement of a first class manufacturing plant is found in these works. The combined plants give employment to fifteen hundred operatives and expend for labor and material about $15,000 per week.

The officers of the W. C. DePauw Co. are N. T. DePauw, president; C. W. DePauw, vice president; Geo. F. Penn, secretary; Wm. Michels, superintendent.

The DePauw works are the largest in the country, engaged in the manufacture of glass and deserve praise for the skill and executive ability which directs as well as the enterprise which founded this worthy establishment.

WOOLEN AND COTTON INDUSTRIES.

NEW ALBANY WOOLEN AND COTTON MILLS.

VINCENNES AND BEELER STREETS.

The history of all industrial establishments are largely inseparable from their originators, and especially is this the case with the above works, which was incorporated in 1864 by L. Bradley, W. C. DePauw, R. G. McCord and J. M. Haines, with capital stock of $75,000. A practical man, who had knowledge in this special line, was found in the person of J. F. Gebhart, who was the founder of woolen manufacturing in New Albany, and under whose superintendency the plant has been made what it is. The beginning was small and many difficulties were to be surmounted, not the least of which was needed a constant and equable supply of water. Mr. Gebhart realizing the urgent need of an unlimited water supply pushed forward in that direction, and was finally awarded by the formation of the Water Works Co. A full description of which has already been given. The buildings have been replaced and added to from time to time, having been partially burned 1883; the machinery now consisting of the most approved kinds, comprising 18 sets of 60 inch cards and all necessary adjuncts which makes it the largest mill of its kind in the country. The principal products of the mill are jeans, blankets, flannels, cassimeres and army kerseys. The latter is sold direct to Government contractors, and the former products go principally to jobbers in metropolitan cities. The entire output is of superior make, commanding ready sale, and the annual output reaches about $900,000. Some 700 persons, largely females, find employment in the various departments of this immense plant, and the disbursement for wages is widely felt among the populace and merchants of this place.

N. T. DePauw, president, is mentioned in the preceding article.   John F. Gebhart, superintendent, was born in Maytown, Pa., where he learned the weaver's trade with his father.   Later he invested in business which proved unprofitable, and leaving Pa. he determined to retrieve his fortune in the west.   Mr. Gebhart decided that this city presented a good field for manufactories and by his success in the Woolen Mills, Water Works, planning the Belt and Terminal, the Highland Electric, and other railroads of this place as noted elsewhere, has proven that his faith was well founded.   That he should have achieved such distinguished success within 30 years, having started here single handed and without previous acquaintance, is not only evidence of excellent business tact, perseverance and stamina upon his part, but is positive proof that New Albany has the essential features for successful manufacturing.   The unqualified success which the New Albany Woolen and Cotton Mills has achieved is a tribute to the efficiency of the management and a matter in which every citizen of this city should feel a personal pride.

NEW ALBANY HOSIERY MILLS.

EKIN AVE., NEAR VIN. ST.

"Great oaks from little acorns grow."   Likewise many of our large manufactories had their inception in small beginnings.   A Hosiery department was started in the Woolen Mills in May, 1879, as an experiment, and as ready sale was found for the product the business was rapidly increased.   Two years later it was purchased by W. A. Hedden and Richard Greuner and the machinery removed to a rented building corner of Main and State streets.   Suitable buildings, at the present location, were completed and equipped in 1883-4.   Several additions have since been made, the main building being now 50x150 feet with three and four floors and several smaller buildings, all made of iron and brick with metal roofs.

On Jan. 1, 1891, the New Albany Hosiery Mill Co. was organized, as successor to W. A. Hedden & Co , the present plant being one of the most complete industrial establishments around the Falls.   About 175,000 lbs. of wool is annually consumed here.   Four sets of cards, 1,300 spindles, 130 knitting machines, 10 sewing machines a machine shop, smithery, dye house and all the necessary auxiliaries are found. Employment is given to about 150 females, and the funds disbursed greatly assist many an humble home.

J. F. Gebhart, president, is also president of the Woolen Mills, where his personal mention will be found.   Wm. A. Hedden, secretary and treasurer, is a New Albanian in mercantile trade since 1862; largely interested in the business enterprises and real estate of the city.   R. T. Brooks is bookkeeper, and each department is in charge of a trustworthy foreman.   The mills make specialties of the best Shaker socks; also ribbed and fashioned hose, fine gauze and other grades, which are sold to leading jobbers from the Atlantic to the Pacific, and the steadily increasing demand is conclusive evidence of the superiority of product.

COTTON BATTING MILLS CO.

EAST EIGHTH STREET, NEAR VINCENNES.

The above company was organized in 1882, and soon afterwards commenced operations in a small way.   It had a precarious existence until the principal stock as purchased by Lawrence Bradley in 1889, and active measures taken to put the lant in first class condition. For a year or two past it has been using nearly 5,000 ales of cotton annually, most of the time running night and day in order to eep up with the orders. The plant cost $50,000, and has been furnished roughout with the best cotton machinery, a considerable portion of which has een built in New Albany, to special patterns made for this concern. L. Bradley, resident of the above company, was born in N. C. Nov. 25, 1815, and came to New lbany in '30. In 1853 he commended the wholesale boot and shoe trade, nine ears later accepting R. G. McCord as a partner and adding wholesale drygoods to ie business. In 1870 this mercantile house was moved to Louisville, and soon fterward Mr. Bradley retired. He was the leading spirit in organizing the lerchants National and Second National Banks and has been largely interested in ailroad development, having served as director of L., N. A. & C. and Air Line in ieir developing years, and he has been continuously interested in our city's pbuilding. C. P. Gwin, secretary and treasurer, is a native of this city, and has een raised in mercantile pursuits. C. L. Bradley, son of the president, is superin-ndent of the mill. He was educated in the city schools, and has been a lifelong esident of New Albany. The plant covers 2 acres of ground, principally covered ith fire-proof buildings, and the output is $175,000 to $200,000 annually. The ioney paid for wages assists in the general prosperity, and the Batting mills is an ssential addition to the city's manufacturing development.

IRON AND STEEL WORKING INDUSTRIES.
OHIO FALLS IRON WORKS.
WATER STREET, BETWEEN WEST FOURTH AND FIFTH.

Manufacturing enterprises have been largely instrumental in bringing this city to rominent notice. While the mercantile houses of a city give beauty and character to s architecture, it is none the less true that the real strength of a community lies in ıose institutions which furnish employment to labor. The Ohio Falls Iron Works as organized in 1866, with capital stock of $200,000, the buildings and machinery eing ready for operations early in 67. The plant includes four commodious uildings, with excellent river and railroad facilities. The area covered is 400x500 ɛet, a full square, the product being largely merchant bar and bridge iron, car, agon, plow and other dimension iron, which is principally sold to jobbers and ıanufacturers. The K. & I. bridge company and Pennsylvania system give direct ɔnnections with eight trunk line railroads, terminating at this place and Louisville, hich furnishes unexcelled shipping facilities and with a competing water way, ig iron can be secured from the various furnaces of the east, west and south at ıwest possible freight rates. A specialty is made of extra quality bridge iron. his company manufactured the iron used by the Louisville Bridge Co., in bridging he Ohio river between this city and Louisville. The capacity of these works is early 1,000 tons of finished iron per month, employment being given to from 200 to 50 mechanics and laborers, the pay roll ranging from $2,500 to $3,000 per week. 'he constantly increasing patronage of this establishment, is conclusive proof that Iew Albany's manufactories can produce a quality and finish of iron that meets very competition. The enterprising manufacturers of this city, by good business tact, are creating a demand for their products in distant cities and thereby advertising New Albany's advantages as a manufacturing city.

N. T. DePauw, president of the Ohio Falls Iron Works, is president of several other concerns, and is mentioned personally in the article on DePauw Glass Works. Peter R. Stoy, vice president, treasurer and manager, has been superintendent here since 1874; and under his conservative management the business has steadily increased upon a sound basis. Mr. Stoy was born in New Albany Feb. 25, 1825, and has made a long and successful record in mercantile and manufacturing pursuits. He is thoroughly posted in the iron trade, prudent and efficient as a business man. He has for many years been prominently connected in educational and religious progression, and his influence has been widely felt in this city. Walter E. Stoy, secretary, is son of the above, a graduate from the DePauw University and for 5 years past connected with the above works. The directors, in addition to the above are W. H. Lewis, John McCulloch and C. W. DePauw. Frank M. Stoy, a graduate of the High School and N. A. Business College, is travelling solicitor, and Fred. T. Watkins has been the efficient shipping clerk for several years. The above works have contributed a full share towards the manufacturing prosperity of this city and have established a high standard of merit in the markets of the country.

NEW ALBANY MANUFACTURING COMPANY.
WATER STREET, BETWEEN PEARL AND BANK.

W. C. DePauw and Chas. Hegewald originally started the business of this plant in 1874. N. T. DePauw purchased his father's interest about 1880, and continued a partner with Mr. Hegewald until 1889, when the latter withdrew from the concern, and Jan. 1, 1890, a stock company was formed. There are 100 stone quaries along the Monon railroad within 100 miles from this city. Good ledges for building purposes are abundant, and limestone quarries for macadamizing streets and other work are extensively operated. A leading specialty of this establishment is the production of channelling machines, stone saw gangs, hoists, derricks, stone trucks and other machinery found necessary in excavating or handling stone. The foundry has a ten-ton daily capacity and a complete machine shop furnishes the requisites for doing any kind of iron repair work or turning out new machinery to order.

N. T. DePauw, president of this concern, is mentioned many times in our manufacturing pages, as his well known business tact and ample capital has brought him to the head of a number of our successful industrial enterprises. E. C. Hangary, treasurer, is mentioned on page 24, as cashier of Merchants National Bank; R. H. Bailey, secretary, is a native of Louisville, and has been with the New Albany Manufacturing Co. since March, 1890. W. H. Coen, vice president, is a native of Canada, served as manager of the Avery Plow Works, of Louisville, for six years, and was manager of the Woolen Mills, a year prior to assisting in the opening of this factory. He is at present secretary and manager of the Premier Steel Co., at Indianapolis. T. H. O'Donnell, superintendent, was born in St. Louis, Mo., learned the moulders trade in his native city, and has been in charge of various foundries in the Falls cities for 25 years past. To Mr. O'Donnell is largely due the credit of extending the trade among the quarries as he has acquired an intimate acquaintance with their needs, and gives personal supervision to that part of the trade, a portion of each week. Forty to fifty machinists, moulders and laborers find employment here, and this plant is one of the factors which has and is assisting in the progress of New Albany's manufacturing development.

NEW ALBANY RAIL MILL COMPANY,

WATER STREET, FROM W. 5TH TO W. 8TH.

The New Albany Rail Mill Company occupies the front rank among the manufacturing corporations of Indiana, as well in the extent of its plant, the capital employed, and the variety and volume of its products. This immense establishment is also the pioneer in Indiana in the manufacture of rails, as well as in structural iron and sheet iron and sheet steel. The company is composed of gentlemen of large capital as well as of great business energy and enterprise. The president is Charles W. DePauw, and its superintendent and general business manager, Albert Trinler, while in its directory and among its shareholders are both the above named gentlemen, Newland T. DePauw, Peter R. Stoy and Alexander Dowling, all being well known in the business circles of Indiana and the neighboring states. There is probably no stronger firm, either in wealth and business talent and live and liberal energy and enterprise, engaged in manufacturing at any other locality in the West.

The capacity of the plant of the New Albany Rail Mill Company is so extensive as to be equal to any possible demand upon it from the trade of the country. In machinery, equipment of every kind, requisite in a varied manufacturing establishment of this character, the New Albany Rail Mill Company's plant is complete. Its rolling mill department is capable of producing iron rails, through all their grades, in size from the smallest mine and tramway lines to the largest railroad iron; structural iron of every description, of any desired pattern, requisite length and strength; cable road equipments in all their completeness, spikes and fishbars, sheet iron and sheet steel.

Added to these is a large foundry department, capable of heavy production and complete in the detail of its equipment. An extensive smithery is attached to meet any needed demands in forge work. The plant covers three entire blocks or squares, and the machinery occupying the buildings is all first class, of modern construction and of the latest and best invention and model.

With advantages like these, the New Albany Rail Mill Company is able to enter into the most active competition for business with similar establishments throughout the country. There is no competing establishment that possesses superiority over this company in any of the lines of the latter's production. The New Albany Rail Mill Company is a leader in the structural iron market; it is also a pioneer and a leader in the sheet iron and sheet steel, being the only establishment west of Pittsburgh operating a sheet mill on a large scale and of perfect equipment. It is also a pioneer and leader in Indiana in small rails for mines, mills, tramways and street car lines.

Many of the cable roads in the cities of the West have been furnished throughout by the New Albany Rail Mill Company which was the first mill in the West to establish a specialty in the department of productive industry. This was in the early days of cable roads, while the works were under the presidency of the late Hon. W. C. DePauw, a man whose comprehensive business mind took in the importance of this, then new, method of passenger transportation for cities, and he had with him then as superintendent and general manager, Albert Trinler, who still occupies the same business relation to the company.

Mr Trinler has been with the company since its organization, and its first enterprising efforts were put forth to build up at New Albany one of the greatest manufactories in the State. The president of this company, Charles W. DePauw, lacks no element in business sagacity and live, energetic, liberal business push and foresight; and is, withal, a gentleman of thorough information in the iron trade. Mr. DePauw and Mr. Trinler are the active business men of these immense works, and that their management is wise, conservative and in sympathy with the trade is evidenced by the success that has placed the New Albany Rail Mill Company's mills in the front rank among the great industrial establishments of the West.

There is nothing lacking in the plant of this immense iron manufactory to make it complete in every detail. In furnaces, rolls, and other machinery it is perfectly equipped. In its power, obtained from several batteries of boilers and a number of the finest engines, there is never any lack, let the demand upon the several departments be ever so heavy. There are separate batteries of boilers and separate engines for every department.

The New Albany Rail Mill Company finds a market for its products in all parts of the West and South. The company enters these fields without fear of opposing competition, because it possesses the faculties and the capital to successfully meet the most enterprising competitors. As a result of a wise and enterprising policy the company is not only popular with the trade in its several lines of production, but is steadily adding to its plant and its ability for a wider and broader field, even than it now occupies.

CHARLES HEGEWALD COMPANY.
STATE TO W. FIRST, ON WATER ST.

The Chas. Hegewald Co. has a complete outfit of modern boiler making machinery; a well equipped machine shop, a large two cupola foundry, with combined capacity for 25 tons of casting daily, a well established brass foundry, and the company is fully prepared to handle any and all work in the boiler, sheet iron, engine and repair line. A leading feature of the trade handled by this concern, is the building of marine engines and boilers and other steamboat machinery, but all sizes of stationary engines and boilers, shaftings or other machinery or castings are produced to order. Charles Hegewald, president and manager of the above company, is a native of Saxony, Germany, and learned the machinists trade in the fatherland. He came to America in 1853, and a few years later became a workman in a New Albany machine shop. During the war he was foreman of the American Foundry, now a part of the Rail Mill plant, and in 1873 became the senior partner in the firm of Chas. Hegewald & Co. While manager of this concern he made the machinery for the Water Works, a portion of the DePauw Glass Works machinery and assisted in fitting up several of the principal manufactories. He has equipped about 200 boats with machinery. In 1889, Mr. Hegewald withdrew from the old plant and fitted the extensive building of which he is the present manager. A stock company was incorporated Jan. 1, 1890, and named the Chas. Hegewald Co., with capital stock of $30,000. The average annual output is from $150,000 to $200,000, giving employment to about 100 men. Eb. J. Hewitt, secretary of the company, served as bookkeeper with Mr. Hegewald for a dozen years prior to becoming one of the incorporators of this concern, thereby familiarizing himself with every detail of the work. The new company have met with a well merited local trade, and are sending large boilers, sheet iron and other machine work to distant towns in this and southern states.

WEBSTER & PITT.

W. FIRST STREET, BELOW RAILROAD.

For a half century past foundry and machine work has been done in this location. Josiah Johnson was in charge of the New Albany Foundry, as the place was then known, before 1850. Alexander Webster, the present senior partner, was born in the Key Stone State, learned the machinists trade at Brownsville, Pa., and came to New Albany in 1848. He worked at the machine business here and in Louisville for a dozen years before engaging as a partner with Mr. Johnson, in 1860. The firm style continued to be Johnson & Webster until about the time of the decease of Mr. Johnson, in 1876, when it became Webster & Pitt. The senior Pitt was connected with the iron business here for nearly fifty years, and Wm. H. Pitt has owned the Pitt interest since the decease of his father, in Feb. 1889. Wm. M. Mix, a native of this place, who has had a varied experience in foundry and machine work, is bookkeeper. Mr. Pitt occupies a prominent position in the machine department of the Woolen Mills.

This plant is thoroughly fitted for foundry and machine repair work, which is a very necessary adjunct to a manufacturing city. The pattern shop has a very complete equipment; the foundry is equal to every requirement; machine department up to the times, and repairs or new work are turned out promptly. The plant fronts 150 feet on W. First street, extending back to the alley. makes a specialty of crushers for cement mill work and fire fronts for Louisville boiler works; also doing any desirable work in the machine or foundry line, to the order of customers, and furnishing regular employment to about 25 skilled workmen.

M. ZIER & CO.

BOILER AND SHEET IRON WORKS.

The late Michael Zier, father of the present proprietor, who died Feb. 24, 1890, commenced the boiler and sheet iron business with Mr. Stuckey, under the firm name of M. Zeir & Co., in 1863, the present M. Zeir having been brought up in the business. The plant was established on the grounds now occupied, corner of Pearl and Oak streets, in Sept. 1890, Dr. E. B. Zier, of Minneapolis, Minn., becoming a partner, with his brother, in this business, March 1st, 1891. The works have a thorough equipment of boiler machinery, and are fitted for all the requirements of sheet iron and steel work. In the year just passed more than a dozen steamboats were fitted with iron work, smoke stacks and other supplies. The senior partner, who has had a life long experience in the works, gives his personal attention to the selection of material and production of goods, the concern giving steady employment to some 40 or 50 mechanics in turning out the special requirements of customers. An establishment of this character is not only an important factor to New Albany, by its disbursement of funds for labor, etcetera, but assists in making the production of equipments required in the fitting of manufacturing plants complete, and adds to the advantages of this place as an industrial center.

IRWIN & MILLHEISER.

CORNER OF SPRING AND WEST FIRST STREETS.

To complete the ornamentation of fine machinery, and in many other directions, a well equipped brass foundry is necessary. This can be found in New Albany in the ORNAMENTAL BRASS WORKS conducted by the above firm. Brass castings were formerly made by Alexis Lemmon, on the site now occupied by the Government building. The present site at the corner of Spring and W. First, was purchased by Irwin & Millheiser, in Oct. 1889, and fitted for all the requirements of brass work. The firm makes all descriptions of brass castings and brass advertising signs. Placques, tiles, &c., are cast in bas-relief from real bronze metal. Car bearings, engine brasses, gaskets, brands, bells, etc., are turned out to the order of customers, and Babbit metal manufactured to meet the requirements of the trade. The partners are natives of this place, Jas. F. Irwin, a graduate of the N. A. Business College, having been for many years connected with the ferry boat trade conducted by his father. Edward Millheiser has had more than a dozen years experience in foundry and brass work. He was for some years connected with the Williamson Art Metal Works of Louisville, serving for a time as foreman, and, for three years prior to opening the present plant, had charge of the Hegewald foundry. All the brass work for the Highland Electric Railway and many other important jobs have been turned out from the above plant. Single journal brasses for the Rail Mill plant, weighing 250 pounds each, and giving entire satisfaction, have recently been produced by this firm.

WOOD WORKING INTERESTS.

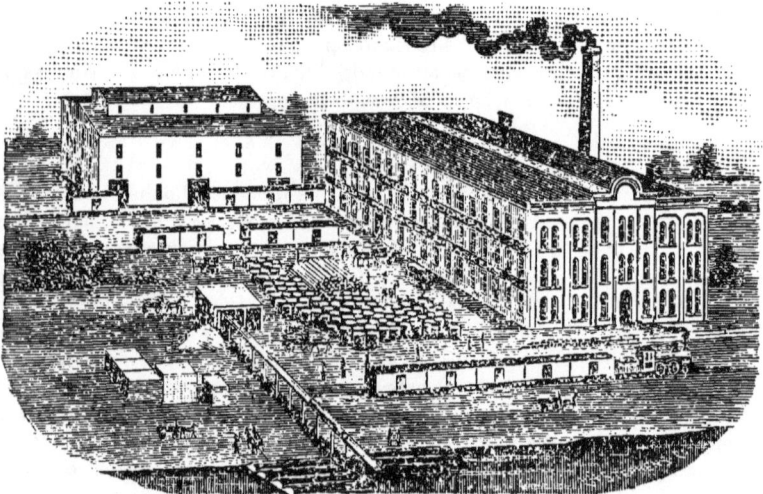

HEATH-MORRIS COMPANY.
FRUIT PACKAGES, BASKETS, ETC.

The above line of manufacture was commenced by Smith, Young & Co., on Main street, about a dozen years since, and later was operated on Market street. The business was purchased by W. R. Heath in 1886, and W. F. Morris engaged as a partner a year later. The trade rapidly increased, and as the firm was compelled to have additional room, the present commodious quarters on Water street, between W. First and W. Second streets, was secured, thoroughly fitted with improved machinery and occupied in 1888. Their patents and mechanical devices cover a wide range in woodworking apparatus, and enable them to turn out 3 or more car loads of complete fruit packages daily. Many of the machines have been perfected and pattented especially for this firm. The establishment is reputed to be the largest of the kind in the United States, operating in their varied line of trade, and its products are shipped extensively to jobbers in nearly all of the middle and Southern States. The plant is connected with the principal railroads by side tracks in the rear, and fronts on the river within one block of the New Albany wharf boat. All sizes and kinds of fruit packages and baskets are made, from pints to two bushels in size, and suitable for berries, cherries, currants, grapes, peaches, vegetables, etc. The timber used is poplar, beech, elm, linn and cottonwood, all easily secured in this section of country. A warehouse 60x120, three stories in height, also connected by railroad, is kept at the corner of Thomas and East streets, shown in the above cut.

Wm. R. Heath, who has the general management of this extensive manufactory, is a native of Benton Harbor, Michigan, in which city he was formerly in the same line of trade for 12 years, and brought a practical knowledge in basket manufacturing, which assists in the permanency and increasing success of the business here. W. F. Morris, who is a native of this county, and a graduate of the New Albany Business College, has been in manufacturing pursuits from boyhood. He is superintendent of the mechanical work, and is familliar with all its details. Owned by practical men, who will make every reasonable effort to keep pace with the demands of the times, there is no perceptible reason why the fruit packing business should not be well cared for by the above works. Upwards of 120 men, women and children are almost continuously employed by this industry, and the extensive fruit growing interests of Floyd and adjacent counties, find a great convenience in securing their packages in the immediate vicinity of where their fruit is grown. After supplying the local trade these works have a large surplus capacity, and as before intimated, their packages find ready sale in the notable fruit and vegetable growing sections of the South and West. These varied industries are each a spoke in the wheel of New Albany's manufacturing development, and the success in any one line is an essential factor in the great aggregate of our industrial importance.

JOHN SHRADER, SR.—FURNITURE, ETC.

FACTORY, W. FIRST—STORE, 11—13, W. MAIN.

The well to do men, of New Albany, have largely accumulated their wealth in this city, and among the self-made men of the place, John Shrader, sr., takes a high rank. Born in Germany, he located in New Albany in 1837, and 9 years later commenced in the furniture and cabinet maker's trade, the business continuing to increase, in 1861 he erected a large factory on State. After this burned, in 1867, he erected and equipped his extensive manufactory, on W. First street between Main and the railroad. The buildings are of brick and fitted for the production of all grades of furniture, from the common to the superb, although principal attention is given to the manufacture of bedroom suites and wardrobes, which are shipped to the southern states. The factory gives employment to over 50 hands, and has been for seven years past, in charge of Jas. H. Gimnich, an expert cabinet maker. The ware and sales rooms occupies the 3 stories and basement, brick block at Nos. 11-13, W. Main street, is filled throughout with furniture and undertaking goods, together with an extensive line of carpets, curtains and house furnishings. Mr. Shrader was a prominent member of city council for 3 terms, and is a stockholder in several of our leading corporations. He has acchieved an enviable success as a business man and citizen of New Albany. He also owns the livery business at Nos. 16–18, W. Main street, which is in charge of his son, Geo. B. Shrader.

FURNITURE FACTORY OF H. KLERNER & SONS.
CORNER OF OAK AND E. FIFTH STREETS.

The above business was started in 1874, and the factory erected in 82 and 85. Walnut, ash, oak and cherry abound in this section, and hardwood bedroom sets and wardrobes is the product, which is principally sold in the south. Over 60 men are employed and the establishment is among our solid manufacturing concerns.

I. F. FORCE—HANDLE FACTORY.
WATER ST., 10TH TO 11TH.

As early as 1848 John Force began the handle business in Rochester, N. Y., and in 1872 the plant was removed to New Albany, Ind., as hickory timber was more easily secured in this section, since which time the business has been conducted by his son, I. F. Force. Much care has been taken in the selection of timber and perfecting the process of manufacture, and the product of this factory is widely known throughout the U. S. and Canada. Mr. Force is engaged in manufacturing in his native city, Rochester, N. Y., and the business here has, for the past 5 years, been in charge of F. W. Peters, of Michigan, who has been with this plant since its establishment in New Albany. Some 60 hands are given employment, a full assortment of handles are constantly kept on hand, and this industry is an important factor in New Albany's continued success and manufacturing development.

NEW ALBANY BENDING WORKS.
EAST MAIN, ABOVE VINCENNES ST.

This plant was started in 1885 by B. K. Taylor, in a small way; purchased in Sept. 89, by the Parry Manufacturing Co., of Indianapolis, since which it has been thoroughly fitted with modern machinery and its capacity increased 400 per cent. Employment is given to some fifty men and the annual output ranges $100,000 or more in value. The concern is one of the leading industries in its line in Southern Indiana, and is exerting an important influence in New Albany's material growth.

I. B. FRIEND—PLANING MILL, ETC.

CORNER OF PEARL AND OAK.

The builders supply line, is a prominent one in any progressive city, and the planing mill, sash, door and blind factory of I. B. Friend is complete in its advantages for furnishing any desirable product of wood finishing, including every variety of turning, scroll sawing, mouldings, sashes, doors, blinds, posts, railing, etc., which are kept in stock, or made to any special design at the order of customers.

This plant was started, in 1856, by John C. Howard. Mr. Friend had located in New Albany in 1849; learned the steamboat cabin building, and later became foreman for Mr. Howard. In 1866 he purchased a half interest and 3 year later became sole proprietor. The boiler of this plant was made by M. Zier & Co., and the engine by Webster & Pitt, thereby showing New Albany facilities for fitting up complete manufacturing establishments. Mr. Friend has erected many of New Albany's prominent buildings, and has done considerable work in Louisville as well. He is at present one of Floyd County's Commissioners and is recognized as a gentleman of energy and enterprise.

GEO. HELFRICH, SR.—PLANING MILL.

S. E. CORNER E. 5TH AND OAK STREETS.

The lumber yard and planing mill of Geo. Helfrich, sr., was established at the above corner in 1881; the mill being fitted for the planing and dressing of lumber of which a good quantity is annually turned out to the order of customers. Mr. Helfrich is a native of Germany, coming to this place in 1848. For 16 years prior to engaging in this business, he served as master car-builder, at the Monon shops, and is well and favorably known to the people of New Albany.

THE HOOSIER PLANING MILL.

S. E. CORNER EAST THIRD AND OAK STREETS.

R. C. Wayman, a Kentuckian, established the above plant some 15 years ago. The buildings are fitted with planers, boiler, engine, etcetera, and is in perfect working order. It is located on a convenient corner, fronting 60 feet on Third street and 120 on Oak, and has a capacity for doing a good trade; but Mr. Wayman, being well advanced in years would accept a young partner, or sell the entire interest at low figures to any person desiring to engage in this line of business.

HOSKINS & KIRWAN—SAW MILL.

RIVER BANK, 7TH TO 8TH STREETS.

The saw mill is almost a necessity to civilization, and certainly lays the foundation for architectural development. Clark & Ogle erected the mill on the river bank adjoining the water works in 1883. This was purchased by W. H. Hoskins Apr. 91, and three months later M. J. Kirwan became a partner. Both the partners are from Louisville and experienced lumbermen. The plant turns out about 20,000 feet a day; but as the business outlook is favorable, the proprietors will put in a modern band sawing output the coming Fall, which will more than double the present capacity. About 30 men find employment with this firm, and the mill is a great convenience to builders, as it promptly cuts to order any requirement not found in the stock of the lumber yards here. The logs are principally secured from the Big Sandy and other rivers flowing into the upper Ohio, which are brought down in rafts and elevated, from the water's edge to the saw carriage, by the usual mill machinery. Lath, etc., are made here, and a good quantity of lumber and other builders material is kept in stock. The mill also has a planing outfit in connection. Although a young firm here, Messrs. Hoskins & Kirwan have displayed an amount of push, enterprise and tact which marks them as successful business men.

I. F. FORCE—HARDWOOD LUMBER.

OFFICE, 14TH AND DEWEY STS.

The most extensive lumber yard in New Albany, is that of I. F. Force, who also runs the handle factory. This is confined to hardwood, including poplar, and keeps in stock about 3,000,000 feet, the handlings of last year running over ten million feet. Mr. Force controls the R. E. Stapp saw mill at the foot of 16th street, owns a mill at Bedford, and several mills in this and other states. The lumber yard here covers a square and a half between Main and Dewey, above 14th street, and is principally engaged in wholesaling, although it has a good local retail trade. It has been for some time past, in charge of A. M. Young, who has served with Mr. Force for 20 years.

NEALY & SHRADER—LUMBER YARD.

ELM, CORNER FIFTEENTH—R. R.

Hugh Nealy, a native of Harrison county, has for 10 years been connected with the lumber trade of this city, and in the spring of 1889, together with L. I. Shrader, formerly in the shoe trade of New Albany, opened the above lumber yard. The plant is directly adjoining the railroad, and the firm, by special care have selected a choice assortment of white and yellow pine lumber, and other requirements for builders use. Large storage sheds are filled with dressed and matched lumber. Railroad transportation has made such wonderful progress that it is now practical to secure shingles from the distant cedar forests of the recently admitted state of Washington, and the best variety of these are sold by the above firm at $4 per thousand.

Louis Bir has for 8 years past kept a well appointed lumber yard, and B. F. Cline has been in the trade for nearly 20 years.

MARBLE, GRANITE AND STONE CONTRACT WORK.

EDWARD CRUMBO, STONE CONTRACTOR.

PEARL ST., OPP. L., N. A. & C. FREIGHT DEPOT.

The successful working of building stone adds greatly to the beauty of architectural development and the solidity of vast enterprises. Edward Crumbo is an acknowledged leader in this line, in New Albany, and many of the prominent buildings and bridges, in this vicinity, have been erected under his superintendence. Among enterprises of special magnitude, may be mentioned the piers and abutments for the K. & I. Bridge Co., and the Belt & Terminal R. R., the Pearl street bridge across Falling run, the Goodbub, Losson, Briggs and other building fronts. Henry Crumbo, father of the above, learned the stone cutter's trade in Germany, and coming to New Albany, in 1845, five years later he engaged in the business, continuing until 1860. Edward Crumbo and Joseph Melcher commenced business, as Crumbo & Melcher, in

1870. This firm was dissolved, by mutual consent, in 1889. Mr. Crumbo continuing the business at the above site, on Pearl street, near Falling run, where he occupies grounds 190x200 feet, which are intersected with switches, connecting with all lines of railroads entering the city; fitted with derricks and equipped for expeditious handling of the most ponderous stones. Mr. Crumbo, being a practical stone cutter of 30 years experience, and more than 20 years in contract work, enables him to undertake and carry to successful completion contracts of any magnitude. A large stock of building stone from Bedford and other desirable quarries, as well as approved marble and granite, are always kept in stock, many of the fine monuments and other cemetery work in this vicinity coming from his establishment. Born in Germany and brought to this city in childhood, he has been deeply interested in New Albany's success, has served in the city council, and is prominently connected in the social and benevolent orders. All kinds of plain and ornamental stone work are turned out by this concern, the elegant new school house, on Vincennes street, now going up under Mr. Crumbo's supervision; who has greatly added to New Albany's Architectural development. He gives employment to about 50 men, thereby largely assisting in the continued success of the city.

JOHN VERNIA & CO.—MARBLE AND GRANITE WORKS.
CORNER OF PEARL AND ELM STREETS.

The business of this house was started in 1876 by John & Frank Vernia, the firm name continuing the same style, since the decease of the junior partner, in 1888. John Vernia was born in Lafayette twp., this county, learned the marble trade with Prof. Brown some 27 years ago, and our cemeteries have a full share of handsome monuments which are the direct product of his handiwork. In his works, corner of Elm and Pearl streets, can be found a great variety in marble and granite work of both domestic and imported stone. Mr. Vernia also handles building stone for cemetery lot fencing, and gives steady employment to from 10 to 12 men.

MELCHER & HERLEY—STONE AND MARBLE WORKS.
CORNER FIFTEENTH AND POPLAR STREETS.

The late Joseph Melcher was engaged in the stone contract work, in this city, from 1870 until his decease May 1, 1891; having been a member of the firm of Crumbo & Melcher, until that firm was dissolved, by mutual consent, in 1889. In 1890, he accepted as a partner Wm. S. Herley, an experienced stone cutter, and since Joseph Melcher's death, that interest has been in charge of his son Chas. F.; who is a graduate of the N. A. Business College, and has taken a course of instruction in the Polytechnic Institute of Louisville. The partners are natives of New Albany, and the yards turn out all kinds of stone, marble and granite work, taking contracts for building fronts, or anything in that line. The plant adjoins the Monon tracks at 15th and Poplar, and furnishes employment to from 10 to 20 men.

E. F. SMITH—MARBLE AND GRANITE.
SEVENTH ST., AT CEMETERY.

E. F. Smith, a native of Strassburg, France, in New Albany from childhood learned the stone cutters trade in this city, and has been engaged in the business for 16 years past. He turns out everything desirable in the monumental line and cemetery work. Mr. Smith has erected some of the best work in the Northern Cemetery, among which are Bradley, McCord, Moore, Humphrey, LaFollette, and other monuments. Several men are employed under the personal supervision of the proprietor.

ANDREW SCHMITT—STONE AND MARBLE WORKS.

NO. 412, E. MARKET, AT R. R.

Andrew Schmitt, of German descent, was born in Pittsburg, came to this vicinity in childhood, learned the stone cutter's trade with Crumbo & Melcher over 20 years ago, and commenced business with Wm. Herley as Herley & Schmitt in 1882. After 10 years he purchased his partner's interest, continuing the business on Market street, adjoining the L., N. A. & C. R. R. Mr. Schmitt contracts for stone building and all kinds of cemetery work, and his experience in the business has brought him a fair share of the trade in that line.

Prof. J. Brown has conducted a prominent marble shop at corner State and Elm for nearly 40 years past.

LEATHER MANUFACTURING INTERESTS.

THE DAY LEATHER COMPANY.

CORNER OAK AND E. 4TH STREETS.

The leather industry of New Albany should not be overlooked, in reference to our importance in manufacturing, as many thousands of hides are annually purchased here, and large quantities of leather shipped. The late Theodore Day, father of the present members of the above company, commenced the tanning business in this city 54 years ago, and the Day Brothers have been brought up in the trade, thereby receiving all the advantages of experience. The company was incorporated in 1883; A. T. Day officiating as president; John I. Day, vice president, and Chas Day, secretary and treasurer. The tannery, located at the n. w. corner of Oak and E. 4th streets, is fitted up with all necessary machinery and appliances for the production of first class oak harness leather, making a specialty of heavy hides, of which about 15,000 are turned out annually. This is shipped to jobbers all over the Union, giving entire satisfaction. It is a noteworthy fact that this establishment has not shut down, from any cause, for a consecutive week, in the past 35 years; but gives constant employment to about 35 men, and the standard regularity of goods produced by the Day Leather Co. is so well known among harness men, that no salesman is required on the road, the orders coming direct to the tannery.

BARTH'S TANNERY.

E. 10TH, ON RIVER.

The very extensive tannery of A. Barth is located on E. Tenth, between Beeler and Water streets. It was established, in 1864, by A. Barth & Co; Mr. Barth becoming sole proprietor in June 85. The tannery and appurtenances cover about an acre of ground comprising six well fitted buildings, with an annual capacity of 15,000 to 20,000

OF NEW ALBANY, IND.

hides. Mr. Barth has had a life long experience in the business and manufactures all grades of leather, although his principal attention is given to harness leather.

GEORGE MOSER & COMPANY.

NO. 272 TO 278 E. 8TH STREET.

This plant was originally started, in 1840, by Lockwood Brothers; purchased by George Moser, Jan. 1, 1878, John M. Moser becoming a partner in July, 91. George Moser is a native of Germany, and commenced the tanner's trade with A. Barth & Co., some 25 years ago, while J. M. Moser is a native of New Albany. The firm have a well fitted tannery, and handles about 15,000 hides of medium weight annually the leather being tanned with chestnut oak and suitable for the use of harness and collar makers. The Moser tannery has a well earned reputation and its products find ready sales among jobbers in various parts of the country. Some 30 to 35 men are employed in this industrial concern.

A. Hopkins & Son have recently overhauled the tannery at the corner Cherry and West streets, for the production of seating leather from hog skins. They also handle about 500 tons of sumach annually. R. Wunderlich runs a tannery on E. 8th street. and two other tanneries are controlled by A Barth.

INDIANA BREWING COMPANY.

CORNER MAIN AND WEST STREETS.

This plant was started in 1881, by Louis Smith; Jacob Horning becoming proprietor the next year. The concern was made an incorporated company, with authorized capital of $100,000, in May, 89, and under the executive care of Gustav Weinmann, was largely increased in order to meet the demands of customers. On an adjoining lot the company have a nest of 24 two-inch wells, put down for the supply of pure water. The brewery grounds are 120x360 feet, upon which, in addition to the large original plant, a handsome 5-story brick structure, which makes a decided improvement to the architectural development of this section of the city, has recently been completed. This has been equipped with the most approved machinery and appliances, no expense having been spared to perfect plans for the manufacture of the best product in this line. The floors are laid of ashphalt and granitoid, and are the most perfect to be found in the city. The plant is traversed on three sides by the principal railroads entering the city. The process of manufacture may be of interest to the general reader, and we will rehearse it in brief. The malt is taken by elevator to the cleaning reel, on 5th floor, where sprouts or other foreign substances are removed, from whence it goes to the malt bin; when needed it is run to the scale hopper, thence through a crusher, and is carried by elevator to the meal hopper, thence to the huge mash tub which holds 150 barrels. Here it undergoes a steeping process for several hours, when the infusion is drained, through pipes, into an immense brass kettle, holding 150 barrels, while the refuse malt is lowered into a receptacle, from whence it is sold for dairy feed. In the brass kettle the propper addition of hops is made, after which it is boiled for 3 or 4 hours. It is then passed through a strainer, and from thence, by pumps, the liquid is raised to an immense surface cooler, on the 5th floor, from which it descends over a system of copper pipes, which are constantly cooled by flowing ice water, and is eventually carried to the storage tubs, of which there are 30; holding 40 barrels each. Subsequently the beer is conducted to the storage cellar, where about a hundred huge casks are found, ranging from 1,200 to 2,400 gallons each in capacity. Here the temperature is kept at 32 to 34 degrees and after 4 months the product is sufficiently matured to barrel and ship to the trade. The ice machine, having a ten-ton capacity, is kept running night and day, and is one of the best congealers in this section of the country. The two large boilers are of New Albany manufacture, one coming from the works of Chas. Hegewald & Co., and the other bearing the marks of M. Zeir & Co. A goodly number of men and teams are employed here, and large quantities of beer is bottled to order. The annual capacity is about 25,000 barrels, and the product finds ready sales in New Albany and surrounding towns.

Gustav Weinmann, the president and manager of the company, is a native of this city, who has been engaged in our manufacturing industries since his graduation from the New Albany Business College in 1881. He became connected with this plant in May, 83, and under his management the establishment has grown to be one of the foremost breweries in this section of the country. Frank Zoeller is the city salesman, and his ability is attested by the large daily sales, while the manufacture of beer is under the supervision of Moritz Eck, as foreman, who learned his trade in the large brewing establishments of Germany.

CITY BREWERY.
CORNER W. FOURTH AND SPRING STREETS.

John Jager erected a brewery on this location about 1840, which was later purchased by Metcalf, of Louisville. Paul Reissing had learned the brewing and malting business in Germany, and in 1857 he leased this place, four years later purchasing it. The plant has been remoddled and refitted from time to time until it is now thoroughly modernized. This establishment manufactures its own malt, and the beer here produced is brewed on a process which brings out its best qualities. With a large capacity ice machine, the proper system of coolers and a complete malting establishment, the plant is well equipped for the production of lager, and 10,000 to 12,000 barrels find annual sale from this concern, principally in New Albany and surrounding cities. Some 15,000 bushels of barley is purchased annually. A dozen to fifteen men find employment here, and the City Brewery from its 50 years of continuous operations has secured a well established custom. Mr. Reising a few years since associated with himself in the business, his son-in-law, Fred C. Kistner, a popular young man, possessed of business tact and energy, and who now practically has the entire management of the plant.

NEW ALBANY STEAM LAUNDRY.
31, EAST MAIN STREET.

Laundry work can hardly be called manufacturing, and yet from the machinery used, and the employment given to labor, it should properly be classified in the department of industry. In the perfection of its machinery, the magnitude of work, and the general accommodation to the public, the New Albany Steam Laundry stands among the first, and has become justly popular under the present management. The rooms are large, light and convenient, fitted with engine and boiler, in the rear, a reversible steam washer, of the latest pattern; suction wringer, that removes the water from the linen without the least injury to the fabric; a shirt ironer, collar and cuff ironer, machine for dampening and folding a lay-down collar, without danger of cracking the goods, and a polisher and curler to finish collars and cuffs to the wearer's satisfaction. This business gives employment to about a dozen persons, the average monthly wages adding its mite to New Albany's improvement. Although doing work as low as any other establishment of its kind, the proprietor, by personal industry, is able to pay his bills and is fully satisfied with his first year in this establishment. O. D. Barras, proprietor, is a native of Saratoga, N. Y., and has spent 9 years in the laundry trade, having been at Canton, Ohio, for four years, prior to the purchase of this plant last year.

SEYMOUR'S AMERICAN LAUNDRY.

NO. 84, E. MARKET STREET.

Cleanliness is said to be next to godliness, and a great improvement has been made within the present generation in regard to laundry work. By former methods, our mothers fretted and stewed, to get the son's linen in presentable shape before the time of going to see his best girl. Now all this is trusted to the laundry, where a scientific reckoning has been made of bleaches and polishes, and the labors of the home are thereby very much lightened. Phillips & Seymour, believing there was room for another first class laundry, in Aug. 1891, opened the above establishment, which has rapidly grown in public favor, and at present has a large line of trade among our best families. The washing is done by hand, as it is believed that this method wears the fabric less, but machinery is used for ironing shirts, collars, cuffs, etc., and every care is taken to meet the wants of the most fastidious. March, 92, Jos. S. Seymour, who has but just attained his majority, but possessed of business enterprise, purchased the interest of his partner, Eugene Phillips, and is now the sole proprietor. The services of 8 to 10 persons is required in this new establishment and the proprietor is well pleased with his opening success.

GILMORE'S CRYSTAL LAUNDRY.

NO. 67, BANK STREET.

The Crystal Laundry was started by M. E. Gilmore, a native of Green Castle, Ind., in 1885, who by a careful study of his customer's wants has secured a large line of patronage. Care is taken to avoid unnecessary wear to the goods and with skilled help, the necessary machines for ironing, polishing, etc., the linen is turned out in a very acceptable style. This laundry gives employment to 10 or 12 hands, does work at the lowest rates, and is among our established industrial concerns.

(*Manufacturing Interests continued on a subsequent page.*)

THE OHIO RIVER INTERESTS.

To the river trade, New Albany owes her origin, her early development and her principal growth up to the middle of the present century. Many of the fleetest and finest boats that have navigated the Ohio and Mississippi were built in the ship yards of this city. In the 20 years prior to the war the total cost of boats built at New Albany was over eight millions of dollars. The gunboat Tuscumbia, built here in 1863, cost the Government $150,000, and in 1864-6 more than a million dollars worth of boats were completed at this place, but a depression in trade coming on then, and the principal attention of capitalists having turned to railroads about that time, the boat building interest here was practically suspended. Waterways all over the republic are rising in popular estimation, as they assure cheap transportation of freights to competing points and are gaining favor as a convenient method of travel, for health and pleasure. The great commercial interests of the West and South are becoming more marked each year, and as New Albany has the best natural location for boat building, an energetic company, with a moderate amount of capital, and a proper display of enterprise, could restore the ship yard business to its former importance. The best oak timber is to be found in this section; the location is just below the Falls where it never suffers from low water in the summer, nor ice in winter. We have the foundries and machine shops for a complete equipment of steamboat machinery, and the best of marine manufacturing sites, which can be purchased at low figures or leased for a term of years at a reasonable remuneration.

LOUISVILLE & EVANSVILLE MAIL LINE.

The competing waterway, furnished by the beautiful Ohio, is a great essential to the Fall Cities manufactories and mercantile houses, and the Louisville & Evansville Mail Co. is of special advantage to this city in many ways. It furnishes a daily line of mail for all the river towns, carries Adams Express, a full line of freights and has elegant passenger accommodations. One of the steamers—Tell City, City of Owensboro, or James Guthrie—starts from the Louisville wharf at 4:30 every week day, leaving the New Albany wharf at 5 p. m., for Owensboro, Evansville, and the lower Ohio towns. The Memphis & Cincinnati packet line connects here regularly on Thursdays and Sundays, and the Southern Transportation Co. also runs a regular line of steamers.

The L. & E. Mail Co. celebrated Washington's birthday by establishing an independent wharf boat here, which is maintained free to all shippers and is supported by the above companies. It is in charge of Steve Green, a native of Brandenburg, Ky., who has been connected with steamboat transportation since 1885, coming from the Grace Morris to the charge of the New Albany wharf boat Feb. 22, 92.

Shippers should not be charged for the privilege of storing goods for transportation by the river, and when some plan is perfected by which wharf boats, like freight houses are maintained by the company or boat receiving the goods, the river will increase in freight business. The steamboat does as much for commercial advancement in proportion to the capital invested as the railroad, and should be properly encouraged; but each boat receiving goods should pay its proportion for wharf maintenance instead of shippers paying a tax for the privilege of sending and receiving goods in this manner.

Col. W. W. Hite. president of the L. & E. Mail Co., has been engaged in the river trade for the past 15 years; his father, Capt. Wm. C. Hite, deceased, having formerly been a steamboat owner, and actively interested in river commerce until his death, when the mantle of business succeeded to the son, W. W. Hite. Louis Hite, also a son of the late Capt. Hite, is secretary. D. L. Penney, superintendent, has had 30 years experience in this trade, and C. E. Hyde, general agent, has charge of the freight business.

FERRY PRIVILEGES, WHARF, ETC.

The first ferry privilege across the Ohio, below the Falls, was granted by the Virginia Legislature to a Mr. Wright, before the commencement of the present century; but little business, however, having been done at this point, prior to the development of New Albany. The Scribners secured from Col. John Paul the right to the ferry privileges here when they purchased the site of this place. After running a somewhat rude ferry for a time, in 1817 they sold the ferry right to Paxon & Smith. John

Conner was early in the business and was succeeded by his son Thomas, the Conners having run the ferry for nearly 40 years. Their interest was purchased by Duckwall & Hunter in 1858. Prior to this an opposition line had been started by Van Sickle & McHarry, but which only continued for a year or two, until a compromise was made. In 1864 Moses Irwin purchased Hunter's interest, and continued as a partner and superintendent until the sale of the ferry boats, Music and Rush, wharfs and prileges to the K. & I. Bridge Co., in 1890 for $70,000. The Rush still continues to make round trips about every 40 minutes, but since the erection of the K. & I. Bridge, a large share of travel goes across that structure, in order to save the incline to the river and steep ascent again to the city level.

Capt. Irwin who was in the ferry trade for over 26 years, is a native of Pa., and resident of New Albany since 1847. Capt. J. B. Mitchell, who was connected with the ferry for nearly 20 years, is a native of Chillicothe. Ohio, where he learned the printer's trade before coming to this vicinity in 1852. He is now connected with the Ledger Co. as secretary.

Capt. Hiram J. Reamer, who has owned the Excelsior wharf boat, at the foot of Pearl street, for nearly 40 years, is a native of Pennsylvania, reared in Ohio, came to New Albany in 1843, served in the Mexican war, and opened the wharf boat business in 1853. As high as 2,500 bbls. of Pork has been shipped from Reamer's wharf in a single day.

PROPOSED CANAL FOR POWER.

As early as 1804, a company was organized for the purpose of buiding a canal around the Falls, on the Kentucky side, and a survey was made. In 1810 Congress passed an act authorizing $150,000 to be raised by subscription, and other acts were passed to forward the project, but no practical work was done until 1825, when Philadelphia capitalists, aided by the Government, undertook the work and the canal was formally opened for traffic Dec. 1830. It proved to be a profitable venture, bringing in tolls enough to pay a good interest on the investment. This canal was enlarged in 72, and made free of tolls.

The Indiana Legislature, in 1819, incorporated a company to make a canal from above Jeffersonville to the river below the Falls. Sufficient subscription had not been realized when successful work had been commenced on the opposite shore, and the scheme was abandoned. This plan has been revived and talked about at different times since and on Dec. 6, 1848, the Indiana Canal Co. was incorporated with authorized capital of $500,000. The plan of this company was to make a boat canal, partly in the river, around the Falls on the Indiana side. Surveys and estimates were made, but the project was finally given up.

With the development of electrical science and water power system, there is abundant reason why a canal should now be bnilt for power purposes alone. Actual figures of cost cannot be given until a survey has been made, but the project appears to be eminently feasible and the investigations of the writer lead to the conclusion that good dividends could be secured on an investment of a million dollars while the indirect benefits from the rise of real estate and advance in manufacturing development consequent thereon, can hardly be overestimated.

We have obtained reports from the principal cities of the East where water power has been developed extensively, and find that (Lockport, N. Y., where the State canal furnish a great surplus excepted,) the lowest rate charged is $20 per annum, for each horse power, on a basis of 10 to 12 hours daily use; and with a development of 10,000 horse power, we would have $100,000 annual rent at half the above rates, which would give 10 per cent. dividends on a million dollars of investment. Holyoke, Lowell and Lawrence, Mass.; Manchester, N. H.; Lewiston, Me. and Columbia, S. C., have each more than 12,000 horse power development, and largely owe their progress and manfacturing success to this fact. Augusta, Ga.; Bellows Falls, Vt.; Cohoes and Rochester, N. Y., with canals ranging from 6,000 to 10,000 h. p. have made wonderful strides in manufacturing development, while New Albany, more centrally located, in first class connection to secure all raw materials, with the best of transportation to reach the markets of the world, and with an undeveloped water power of many thousands of h. p. going to waste at her side, may be said to be lying supinely at her ease, waiting for something to turn up—for the outside world to rush in and thrust greatness upon her—when manifestly the sensible thing to do is to harness the Ohio above the Falls and have it do our bidding in a mechanical way. The only posssible objection to development here, is the change of the water stage. consequent upon floods. This difficulty, cannot be entirely overcome, under any proposed system, but even if works were compelled to take a vacation for a week, every year or two from this cause, the amount saved in price of power, would greatly overbalance the disadvantages from delay. Large establishments are generally furnished with a supernumerary steam outfit in order to meet all possible contingencies.

At this stage of proceeding only suggestions can be dropped for deliberation. The water supply for the proposed canal, should be taken above Jeffersonville, cross in rear of that city, pass over Silver creek in an aqueduct and utilize Falling run as a tail race. By this route the distance need not exceed 5 miles, the fall would be 25 feet or more. and the excavation simple throughout most of the route. The bulkhead, through which the water is introduced, is composed of abutments, piers, arches and parapet wall of stone well laid in hydraulic cement. Ten arches governed by a score of gates, all operated by automatic machinery, would be sufficient to control the water entrance. For a 10,000 h. p. about 1,000 square feet of area opening in bulkhead should be provided. A canal 80 feet wide, and 15 ft. in depth, would give a sufficient area. At the aqueduct crossing of Silver creek, a waste-weir with 5 or 6 waste gates should be provided for the overflow, and from thence to Falling run the dimensions of the canal can be reduced one-fouth or more. Until a correct survey has been made no definite figures can be given, but the investigations of the writer lead to the conclusion that this proposed canal with houses to cover the machinery, aside from the right of way. can be completed ready to furnish power for $500.000; which, as before shown, if it furnished power at half the minimum rate charged by canals now in operation, it would pay a dividend of 10 per cent. on a million dollars of outlay, if its developed power could be utilized. These are not mere fancies, but are reasonable deductions from a review of work accomplished elsewhere. The canal at Columbia, S. C., more nearly approaches the conditions here, having been made where Congaree river has a fall of 35 feet, in 5 miles, and although a third wider than the above proportions, with a complete system of locks for steamboats, a considerable of the distance having been blasted through granite, cost only about three-fourths of a million dollars. The bottom of the canal there has an inclination of but one foot to the mile, and yet their estimated power is 13,000 horse, while, without steamboat locks, it would be entirely feasible to drop the incline here 2 feet to the mile, thereby adding great additional power. With the present inventions for transmiting electrical power, the surplus not used by factories along the line as water power proper, could be, through a large electrical plant, reduced to that subtile power and transmitted to any desirable point in the Falls cities. Even the capacity of the entire canal might be used to conduct an immense electrical plant and sufficient power generated to operate all the factories and street car lines of New Albany, Jeffersonville and Louisville. The possibilities can scarcely be comprehended and the quicker a company is organized to make this development the sooner will New Albany take her proper place among the great manufacturing centers of this country. Marcus Ruthenburg, superintendent of the Light, Heat & Power Co., has made a cursory survey and he believes that the most practical channel would be wrought steel pipes of 6 feet in diameter. This plan would be less influenced by the changes in water stage and could be brought to Silver creek, with about 3½ miles of conduit, where an electric plant might be located. From this source our water works could take a supply uncontaminated, in the least, by the sewage of the Falls cities. It has been estimated that a channel of this size would produce 4,000 h. p., and could be laid for $150,000 per mile. Either this or an open canal project, should at once be adopted to utilize the power now going to waste, and build up a metropolitan city at this point.

RAILROAD TRANSPORTATION.

When we review the history of railroads and discover that within the memory of many who are now living, there were no such thing as railroads proper, cars or locomotives, we are struck with intense admiration for the wonderful evolution which has been developed in machinery, coaches, roads and transportation during the past sixty years. Tramways and horse car roads were commenced about the beginning of this century, and as early as 1802, Trevithick took out the first patent "for adapting a steam engine to the powers of locomotion," although Watts is said to have made a model previously. Several other patents were obtained, but none of practical utility, until George Stephenson's "Rocket" was built in 1829, and run from Liverpool to Manchester, England. This, at that time, wonderful locomotive, weighed but 7½ tons, and could draw 44 tons at a speed of 14 miles per hour. In 1830 Peter Cooper built the first American locomotive for the Baltimore & Ohio R. R., and the same year an engine was built by E. L. Miller of New York, for the South Carolina R. R., which, in 1833, had 136 miles of main track and continued for several years to be the longest railroad in America, for prior to 1840 there were but a few short lines built and railroad development had but fairly begun 50 years ago.

LOUISVILLE, NEW ALBANY & CHICAGO R. R.

One of the oldest railroads in Indiana is the Louisville, New Albany & Chicago. The New Albany & Salem Railroad Company was organized on July 8th, 1847, under the act of January 28th, 1842, which authorized private companies to take up any of the unfinished works of the State and complete the same on their account. On Jan. 25th, 1847, an act was passed which granted the railroad company the right to occupy that part of the New Albany & Crawfordsville macadam road which lay between New Albany and Salem. An act was passed on February 11th, 1848, whereby all the rights of the state were relinquished to the company and an extension of the line granted.

The railroad was opened for business from New Albany to Michigan City, a distance of 287¼ miles on July 4th, 1852. This was a very important railroad to the state, extending from the Ohio river to Lake Michigan and the opening of the road was the occasion for much rejoicing all along the line. On October 4th, 1859, the name of the road was changed from the New Albany and Salem Railroad Co. to the Louisville, New Albany & Chicago Railroad Co.

The road was sold under foreclosure of the mortgages on Dec. 27th, 1872, and was bid in by the bondholders. A new company was organized under the old name. On May 5th, 1881, this company was consolidated with the Chicago & Indianapolis Air Line Railway Co., under the name of the Louisville, New Albany & Chicago Railway Co. On the first day of March, 1886, the L., N. A. & C. Ry Co, bought the Orleans, West Baden & French Lick Springs Railway, upon which the right of way had been secured and some work done. The construction of this road from Orleans to French Lick Springs, a distance of 17.5 miles, was completed about April 1st, 1887. The capital stock of this railway company is $300,000 all of which is owned by the L., N. A. & C. Ry. Co. On the 1st day of April, 1886, the L., N. A. & C. Ry. Co. bought and now owns all of the capital stock of the Bedford and Bloomfield R. R. Co., and has operated that road since that time. The capital stock of the company is $600,000 represented by 12,000 shares of stock of a par value of $50 each.

The miles of road now operated are as follows:

FIRST DIVISION.	MILES.	MILES.
Chicago, Ills, to Indianapolis, Ind........................	183.5.	
Michigan City, Ind., to Layfayette, Ind....................	90 5	274.00.
SECOND DIVISION.		
Layfayette, Ind., to Louisville, Ky., ...	203.9.	
Bedford, Ind., to Switz City, (B. & B. branch)............	41.4.	
Orleans, Ind., to French Lick Springs, (French Lick branch,) 17.5		262.8.
Total miles, ...		536.8.

The capital stock of the road is $9,600,000, and its bonded indebtedness $12,800,-000. The road is popularly known as the "Monon," from the name of the town where the Air Line division crosses the old main line. There are extensive stone quarries along the line of the L., N. A. & C. Ry., at Salem, Bedford, Bloomington, Ellettsville, Stinesville, and other places, and the stone produced by them forms an important item of the freight handled. The business of the road is steadily improving and bids fair to far surpass, in 1892, in its gross earnings and net results, that of any preceding year.

Samuel Thomas, president of the road, John Greenough, vice president, and J. A. Hilton, assistant secretary and assistant treasurer, have their headquarters at 80, Broadway, New York, and W. H. McDoel, general manager, W. H. Lewis, secretary and treasurer, S. J. Collins, general superintendent, R. M. Arnold, general freight agent, Jas. Barker, general passenger agent, and Jos. H. Craig, auditor and purchasing agent, have their offices in the Monon Block, Chicago, Ills.

The commercial and manufacturing importance of the city has been largely aided by the steady operation of the Monon shops for the last forty years. The capital employed in this enterprise is not less than $250,000, and the services of some 400 skilled mechanics are required. The amount disbursed for wages and material is from $15,000 to $20,000 monthly, which contributes very largely to the city's success.

About 70 passenger coaches, 100 locomotives and 5,000 freight cars are in use on the L., N. A. & C. R. R. The overhauling and repair work for the entire line is done here. H. Watkeys, for 26 years connected with the N. Y. Central road, is master mechanic, assisted by Harry Delaney, of Philadelphia, who served 7 years with the Baldwin Locomotive works, and 6 years with the Air Line, prior to commencing with the Monon, Feb. 25, 1892. Chas. W. Coller, an Englishman, who has been in R. R. work since 1864, has officiated as master car builder here for 6 years past, having held a similar position with the Hannibal & St. Joe road for many years. His clerical work has been for 3 years past, in charge of Jas. W. Jenner, a native Hoosier, and graduate of the N. A. Business College. An extensive store house and supply department is kept here, and that is in charge of J. A. Strubel, a Kentuckian, who has been with the Monon for 10 years. Chas Roth, of Jeffersonville, who served as a machinist for 24 years, with the J. M. & I., has charge of the shops as foreman. The immense freight depot, at the corner of Pearl and Oak streets, is in chare of Chas. C. Jack, a native of Toledo, O., graduate of Hall's Business College, of Logansport, who served as cashier in the Monon office, at Lafayette, for five years prior to being transferred to New Albany, in Oct. 91. F. H. Kalies, a native of Michigan City, Ind., in railroad work for 10 years past, took charge or the Vincennes st. ticket office in May, 1888. He also sells tickets for the J., M. & I. railroad, which crosses the Monon at this point.

PITTSBURGH, CINCINNATI, CHICAGO AND ST. LOUIS RAILWAY.

In Feb. 1832, an act was approved for the building, by the State, of a railroad between Madison and Indianapolis. This was surveyed in 36, commenced in 38, and completed from North Madison to Edinburgh in 39. It was leased until 41 for 60 per cent. of the gross earnings. The act incorporating the Jeffersonville R. R., was passed Jan. 28, 1846, road surveyed May 48; built to Vienna 27 miles, in 49, and Columbus in 52. This was consolidated with the Madison & Indianapolis road in 1866, under the title of J., M. & I. In 1865, the Clark county plank road bed was purchased and the six miles of connecting link, from Jeffersonville to State street, New Albany, put down at a cost of $152,695.53. July 1st, 1872, an agreement was completed with the Louisville Bridge Co., for crossing the Ohio river at that place, and Louisville became the southern terminus. In 1873, the J., M. & I. system, aggregating 225 miles; was leased by the Pennsylvania Company, and Oct., 1890, this became the Louisville division of the Pittsburg, Cincinnati, Chicago & St. Louis Railway, with division offices at Louisville, which practically gives all the Falls Cities, direct connection with the vast Pennsylvania system. In the year 1891, 1,800,000 persons were carried on the Louisville division, covering 22,324,000 miles without a fatal accident to its passengers. The "Dinkey" trains on this line run between Louisville, New Albany and Jeffersonville every half hour, making the round trip, for the modest sum of ten cents, and are a great accommodation. They begin at 5 a. m., and close service at 12:30 a. m., having aggregated 54,441 trains in 1891.

G. B. Roberts, president of the P., C., C. & St. L., has headquarters at Philadelphia, James McCrea, 1st vice president, Joseph Wood, general manager, and E. A. Ford, general passenger agent, are found at Pittsburg. J. F. Miller, general superintendent has offices at Columbus, Ohio. H. I. Miller, division superintendent, has been a life-long railroad man, and came from Cincinnati & Logansport division to this

charge in March, 1890. Mr. A. Anderson, passenger agent, has offices at Fourth
and Market, Louisville. New Albany has local stations at 5th, 9th, 16th and Vin.
sts. Byron F. Darrah, a Hoosier, for 11 years past in the employ of this company,
came from Vienna to the charge of the State st. ticket office in 1887. Jas. N. Richards
is baggage master and clerk. C. U. Williams, graduate of a Louisville business
college, has been 14 years with the P. C. C. & St. L., and has for 5 years past, been
in charge of the New Albany freight office. He requires six assistants.

LOUISVILLE, EVANSVILLE & ST. LOUIS AIR LINE.

This road, familiarly known as the Air Line, was surveyed in 1871, partly built in
72, after which work was suspended for some time, but its final completion was con-
summated in 1881. The main line, as its name implies, is a very direct route, reaching St. Louis in a distance of 267 miles, which is 56 miles shorter than by any other
route. The branch from Jasper to Evansville is 54 miles, from Cannelton, a
noted coal mining town, to Lincoln Junction, is 22 miles, and from Rockport to
Lincoln Junction adds 17 miles, making the total length of the road, with its branches
360 miles. The L., E. & St. L. is well equipped, passes through the heart of southern
Indiana and Illinois coal fields, where superior block and cannel coal is found, suitable for all purposes of iron and steel production, and general manufacturing, which
enables our industrial concerns to secure coal at reasonable prices, when the upper
Ohio is blocked with ice, or navigation partly suspended on account of low water.
The route also passes through a well timbered section, and several of our woodworking establishments, recieve the bulk of their supplies by this line. A good agricultural region is traversed, the finest clay is found at Huntingburg and Lincoln, excellent
glass rock at Marengo, mineral paint ores at different points, and the important
cities made accessible through the Air Line are numerous. The largest lime kiln
interest in the western country is found at Milltown, on the banks of Blue river,
where is an extensive park, famous as a summer resort and picnic grounds. This
road also has a regular station at the Holiness Camping Grounds, and with the caves
at Marengo and Wyandotte, there is no lack for interesting excursion resorts. When
all the above advantages are taken into consideration, the importance of the L., E.
& St. L. R. R., to this city, can readily be seen. While it has connections with all
railroads centering at Louisville, through the K. & I. Bridge Co., the eastern terminus of the road is at New Albany. The general offices are at Evansville, D. J. Mack-
ey, president; R. A. Campbell, general passenger agent; E. O. Hopkins, general
freight agent, and G. J. Grammer, traffic manager. All of these gentlemen have a
high standing as railroad men. James Montgomery, of Huntingburg, officiates as
general superintendent, and H. R. King, a native of this city, has had charge of the
New Albany freight and ticket offices since the completion of the road. Mr. King is
a graduate of DePauw University and has been in railroad business for nearly 21
years. Morris McDonald, jr., son of New Albany's mayor, is train master.

KENTUCKY & INDIANA BRIDGE COMPANY.

This is an age of progression, and easy transportation facilities are essential to
rapid development, but when a second bridge across the Ohio was proposed, its
projectors were considered visionary. The promoters of the scheme were, however,
men of wealth and perseverance, and April, 1880, Bennett H. Young, St. John Boyle,
Bluford Wilson, Charles Godshaw and E. F. Trabue secured a charter of incorpora-

tion from the Ky. Legislature. March 7th, 1881, Morris McDonald, J. H. Stotsenburg, J. F. Gebhart, J. K. Woodward and J. J. Brown, all well known business men of New Albany, were incorporators on the Indiana side. The capital stock was made $1,700,000; first mortgage bonds $1,000,000, second mortgage $600,000 and first terminal $400,000 were issued. The two million dollars indebtedness, at 5 per cent. annual interest, makes fixed charges of $100,000; but the earnings for 1891 were considerably above the amount required for interest, showing a very gratifying increase in trade for five years. Work was commenced in 1880, and the last section of the bridge completed April 10, 1886. The roadway was opened for travel about July 1st; the railroad completed and traffic opened on the "Daisy Line" in the winter of 1886. The roadway has become the principal way for team communication across the river, and the Daisy cars carried more than a half million of passengers in 1891. No accident worthy of mention, has occurred to any passenger on this line, but on the 5th of January last, Conductor Mahon was killed in Louisville while in the discharge of his usual duties.

The Bridge, of steel and iron, is about a mile in length, crossing the river just below the Falls. From the Vincennes street depot to 1st street, Louisville, is 4 miles, a Y from 29th street leads out 5 miles to Parkland, a suburb of Louisville, and with the New Albany Belt and Terminal, the whole length of the line is 11 miles. A number of railroads which enter New Albany and Louisville use the K. & I. system for terminal and connecting facilities. The New Albany street railway is owned by the K. & I. Bridge Co., and round trip tickets, covering two rides on the street cars, with passage from the Daisy depot to 1st street, Louisville and return, are sold for 15 cents. Trains are run over this route at stated intervals, averaging about 30 minutes, and the Daisy line is a great popular convenience. In connection with the Highland electric, it gives the people of Louisville, the round excursion to the camping grounds of Silver Hills, for the unprecedented low fare of 25 cents.

The general offices of this line are in the Ky. Natl. Bk. building. Col. Bennett H. Young, who has been president of this company since its organization, has won an enviable record as a railroad builder and manager, and is a financier of acknowledged ability. W. F. Grant, vice president, is an extensive leaf tobacco merchant; Chas. P. Weaver, secretary and treasurer, was for several years assistant P. M. of Louisville, and W. R. Woodard, general manager, is a railroad man of extensive experience. J. P. Pulliam, who was educated in the schools of his native city, Louisville, has officiated as freight and ticket agent at the New Albany depots of the K. & I. Co. for 2 years past.

OHIO & MISSISSIPPI RAILROAD.

About the middle of the present century active steps were begun for building a railroad from Cincinnati, on the Ohio, to St. Louis, on the Mississippi river, a distance of 340 miles. This was completed in 1856, since which a line from Shawneetown to Beardstown, Ills., of 228 miles has been added, and the Louisville branch of 57 miles from North Vernon. By a connecting link of 7 miles from Watson to New Albany, the O. & M., through the K. & I. Bridge Co., has direct connection with the railroads of Louisville and New Albany, and furnishes an outlet from this place to the east, west and north. The O. & M. was built a six foot gauge, as 40 years ago that was believed to be more serviceable; but the gauge was reduced to standard in 74.

The general offices are at Cincinnati. John F. Barnard, president and manager;

C. C. F. Bent, superintendent, and W. B. Shattuc, formerly passenger agent of the
A. & G. W., has for 10 years had charge of the passenger department of the O. &
M. R. S. Brown, of Louisville, is southern passenger agent, while H. H. Conway,
of Madison, Ind., who has been for 12 years with this company, has charge of the
Vincennes street ticket depot; Evan Prosser, chairman of the republican county
committee, is city passenger agent, and W. D. Briggs, of Jackson county, for 20
years past in railroad work, officiates as freight agent.

THE BELT & TERMINAL RAILROAD.

The connecting link with the Air Line and other roads, is built on an elevated
track, skirting the river front, and was projected by our townsman, J. F. Gebhart,
the franchise having been sold to the K. & I. Bridge Co., by which it was completed
in 1890. The road is 2 miles in length and with its rights and privileges cost $300,-
000. It adds largely to the conveniences of shipment, and is an important part of
the K. & I. system.

NEW ALBANY HIGHLAND RAILWAY CO.

A very important addition to New Albany's future development was undertaken
by home capital, in the organization of the above company, July 20, 1890. The
ascent from the foot of Spring street, to the summit of the Knobs, is about 200 feet
in one mile, but by winding around the brow of the bluff, the camping grounds, 2 miles
distant, is reached at a grade of about 120 feet to the mile, which is rapidly ascended
by the electric motor cars. This places the beautiful plat of "Silver Hills" in a condition to be easily reached by those who desire residences in this delightful suburb,
and makes the interstate camp meeting grounds a favorite summer resort, not only
by New Albany people, but by the denizens of Louisville, who, for 25 cents, get a
double ride through their own city, and across the Ohio river, are transferred through
New Albany's principal business streets, and by electric power, are carried up and
down the steep bluffs of Silver Hills. This company have an electric plant and a
full equipment of motor cars. During the busy season cars run every 10 minutes.
John F. Gebhart is president; W. W. Tuley, mentioned among attorneys, is secretary
and treasurer, and David Stine officiates as superintendent. The directors are J. F.
Gebhart, Jacob Goodbub, Geo. P. Helfrich, Henry Terstegge, R. E. Burk, Geo. W.
Tuley and Jacob Zinsmeister.

GLENVIEW PARK RAILWAY COMPANY.

Realizing the importance of the surrounding summer resorts, and suburban property, the Glenview Park Railway was incorporated March 10, of the present year, by
a number of New Albany's prominent business men. The capital stock was made
$50,000, and the proposed line is to extend from Main street to Glenview Park, a dis-
tance of about three miles. Electricity will be the motor power, and there is every
reason why the enterprise will be a good investment. The officers are Jonathan
Peters, president; John E. Crane, vice president; Robt. W. Morris, treasurer, and
Evan Stotsenburg, secretary. Such enterprises are needed in every progressive city,
and should receive proper recognition from the powers that be.

STREET RAILWAY SYSTEM.

Seven miles of street railways furnish facilities for reaching the business and
residence portion of New Albany. The system was originally built in 1865, and was

purchased for $35,000 by the K. & I. Bridge Co. in 1887, in order to make its connections more complete. Subsequently about $75,000 was spent in improvements and equipments, the line now making regular connections between the "Daisy" and Highland electric road, and furnishing a very complete car service. It is contemplated to change the system into an electric line in the near future. John F. Gebhart is president of this and the Belt & Terminal.

REAL ESTATE AND INSURANCE—HOMES, STREETS, ETC.

New Albany is conveniently platted, has numerous well built mansions, surrounded by elegant lawns, and handsome homes of less pretensions. What is still better: through the adjunct of building and loan associations, with the natural thrift and economy of its mechanics and laborers; it has a very large number of convenient and well kept cottages, which are owned by the occupants and upon which no rent is paid. The back alleys are nearly all thoroughly paved, so that it takes but little labor to keep them clean and the principal streets are macadamized. A complete sewerage system is contemplated and subsequent paving by brick or asphalt of the principal thoroughfares. Many fine shade trees stretch their protecting arms over the side walks and streets, to keep off the summer rays of the sun, and altogether this may be called a very pleasant city in which to live. There are numerous outing places, in easy range of distance which are mentioned on other pages. In progress and material development of the place, real estate agents should not be overlooked. This class of business requires a large amount of advertising, which brings New Albany into notoriety, and the more liberal agents and owners give easy terms to those who desire to make immediate developments, thereby encouraging the purchase of lots and establishment of homes.

SOUTHWESTERN R. E. AGENCY—LAF. FREDERICK & SON.

NO. 53, E. MAIN, CORNER BANK STREET.

Perhaps no man in New Albany has been exclusively engaged in the real estate business longer, or is more thoroughly acquainted with every portion of the city and its surrounding suburbs than "Laf." Frederick. Mr. Frederick is a native of this county, served as sergeant in the 23d Reg. Ind. Vols., and later was promoted to a captaincy in the 93d Reg. Capt. Frederick commenced the real estate business in New Albany, in 1869, making himself useful in every department of the business, and carefully looking after his customers needs. With 23 years in that interest he has become familliar with every street of the city, and explicit confidence can be placed in his judgment as to values of real estate, or worth of buildings for rent. One of the noted residence streets of New Albany, is Ekin Avenue, on which this agency has a number of choice lots, which from the elevated position commands a magnifficent view of the city and its unsurpassed surrounding natural scenery. A bird's eye view of New Albany, with Silver hills in a semi-circle to the north and west, the bridges that cross the Ohio, the Falls, and the metropolis on the opposite side of the river, are all in range from this fine residential property. The avenue has been macadamized and graveled, lies superb for natural drainage, and several hadsome residences have been erected; among which may be mentioned those of W. D. Keyes, A. C. Neat, W. H. McKay, W. R. Heath, W. S. Applegate and others. The street has a large water main and is lighted by gas and electrity. Street cars run to Ekin avenue and will doubtless be extended through it to Silver Grove. These lots cannot long be had on the present easy terms, as those most favorably located are rapidly being taken. From the special mention made of this property, it must not be supposed that the principal attention of the firm is confined here; as the agency covers a full share of the best property in New Albany, that is on the market, and those who desire to purchase, sell or rent can safely entrust their business to the above firm. Merrill L. Frederick, the son, is a graduate of the New Albany High school, and was in railroad employ for some time before engaging with his father, as a partner, in 1890. Capt. Frederick & Son have convenient rooms, on the corner of Main and Bank streets, and the South-western Real Estate Agency, has for more than 20 years, conducted a prominent business in this city, thereby assisting in the steady growth of New Albany from year to year.

HELFRICH'S SILVER HILLS PLAT.

OFFICE SOUTH EAST CORNER BANK AND SPRING STREETS.

With the development of electrical power, the problem of how to utilize the bluffs adjoining the city on the west, became an easy matter for solution, and the ascent of Silver Hills, formerly a difficult task, is now an excursion pleasure. The available area for handsome residence lots in New Albany, having long since been taken, an outlet to fine suburban residential property was furnished by the completion of the Highland Railway in May, 1891; since which there has been a large demand, and many sales negotiated on the Silver Hills Plat. The grounds rise quite abruptly from the foot of New Albany's principal streets, at Falling run, to a height of over 200 feet, where a gently sloping summit ridge, extends with some intervening depressions; rising again to the height of 400 feet at Mooresville, four miles north of the Ohio. The bluffs and plateaus, accessible from the Highland Railway, have at once become desirable and attractive sites for residences, giving in panorama a magnificent view of the Ohio and the Falls cities, and insuring a pure atmosphere. Several handsome residences have been built along this ascent, within a few hundred feet from the city limits. Carriage and foot paths have been terraced, and the electric railway at all times forms an easy and agreeable mode of access. Many who have heretofore resided in the smoke and dust of Louisville and New Albany are now seeking for building sites here, and the price of lots will doubtless be rapidly advanced. The summit plateau is from 700 to 1,500 in width and about 2,000 feet in length, extending from the water works reservoirs southward to the point, the electric railway continuing to the campmeeting grounds and Scenic Park. This peak overlooks the three Falls cities—New Albany, Louisville and Jeffersonville—also the broad valley of the Ohio, which can be traced in the distance. The second elevated ridge to the west and north, some 200 feet higher than Silver Hills, serves as a protection from wind storms and cyclones to the latter. The breezes of pure dry air are constant, making it cooler in the summer and less liable to chilliness in cold weather, in consequence of its elevation above the fogs and dampness arising from the river. The residents of this plat have all the advantages of city water, electric lights, and light taxes, and avoid the offensive sights of foul gutters and disagreeable odors of the low ground in the manufacturing sections. This is undoubtedly much healthier than the lowlands, and presenting to constant view, a picture of natural scenery, painted by nature's great artist, there can be found no more romantic or beautiful residence plat in all this section of country. Fruits and shrubery grow to perfection here, and elegant homes, abounding in luxury, will doubtless cover these hill sides and tops, in the near future. Philip Helfrich, agent of the above property, has been reared in New Albany, and is prominently connected with the material advancement of the city.

A. HUNCILMAN & SON, 38 SPRING ST.

OWNERS AND DEALERS IN REAL ESTATE.

The progressive dealer in real estate, who advertises the place in which he lives, and seeks for its general development, is a great assistance to the city's upbuilding; as he is not afraid to practice what he preaches. Among those who have been liberal in making improvements for the furtherance of development, Andros Huncilman, who was born and reared in New Albany, is entitled to a full share of credit; for few if any have done more in platting, improving and sale of lots to prospective builders on suburban property. Through his agency the Silver Grove tract was purchased and platted for mayor Morris McDonald; and more than a hundred lots were sold while it was in the hands of Mr. Huncilman. Nine years ago he purchased the five acre homestead at the terminus of Chestnut or Thirteenth street, known as Cedar Bough. This sandy knoll, from which the water flows in all directions, has been divided into 26 lots, 50x125 feet, which are sold for residence property only. A perfect system of sewerage has been put down, several costly residences erected, and the tract will soon be closed out. Jim. J. Huncilman, who became a partner, with his father, in 1890, is a graduate of the N. A. Business College, spent ten years in civil engineer railroad work, in various states, and to the senior partner's experience of 25 years, adds the energy and impulse of youth. The firm makes a specialty of handling choice suburban realty and have for sale or exchange desirable residential, or manufacturing sites, homes, etc., in various portions of the city and surrounding suburbs. In 1889, with J. F. Gebhart and I. S. Winstandley, Mr. Huncilman purchased a 35 acre tract on the north side, partly in the city, forming the North Park Realty Co. This has since been platted by the above firm, and several thousand dollars expended in grading, building sewers and planting shade trees. Through an intersecting branch of Falling run it has excellent advantages for drainage. The principal part of the plat is well elevated insuring good sewer grades and healthy surroundings. The street railway has been extended to the centre of North Park, and cars make direct connections with all Daisy trains, so that persons engaged in business across the river, can reside here and reach their Louisville office in 30 minutes. The distance from our court house is but 1¼ miles, and yet these lots are sold at $6 a foot. A number of neat cottages have been erected on the principal streets and other purchasers will soon build.

Oakwood, at the upper terminus of the Highland railway, elevated 200 feet above the city, in one of nature's own parks, was platted a year since. Several lots have been sold here, some improvements made, and as it adjoins the Holiness campmeeting grounds, on the edge of the great Scenic Park, it makes a very romantic and beautiful location for summer cottages, at all times accessible through the electric cars. Oakwood is rightly named and will doubtless become a popular resort. The reputation of A. Huncilman & Son, for reliable dealings and liberal terms to customers is too well known to need any comment from the historian.

SCHELLER & MUIR'S R. E. AGENCY.

N. E. CORNER SPRING AND VINCENNES STS.

Jas. G. Scheller, a native of this city, engaged in real estate transactions about 4 years ago, and Nov. 91, accepted Ephraim Muir, as a partner. Mr. Muir is a native of Penna., resided in New Albany many years ago, and after an absence of 16 years returned to this city in 1887. The firm have a full knowledge of the city, and by their stirring movements, are securing a fare share of business in their line. In common with others, who are in position to know, they report that property is steadily advancing in values; and while we have had no *booms*—fit word of recent usage to express exaggeration, and inevitable reaction—fortunately for the future, we have a city which can stand upon its real merit, and property, judiciously purchased, has for several years past, almost invariably brought a natural advance, when it again changed hands.

This condition of matters adds to our permanency, more than speculative prices, by which some one must eventually become heavy loosers. The above firm conduct a general real estate agency, and are prepared to satisfactorily transact all business placed in their hands.

W. H. McKAY'S BIG AGENCY.

NO. 67, PEARL STREET.

Among the many instances of success gained in New Albany, Wm. H. McKay is a proper example. Born in Kentucky, reared in Missouri, he located in this city 20 years ago and became a partner of M. C. Browning. His partner was among the victims of the ill-fated steamer Pat. Rodgers, losing his life Aug. 5th, 1874. Three years later Mr. McKay became sole owner of the business, and is now one of the leading underwriters in this section of country. He represents twelve leading companies in fire insurance, his business extending to many towns in southern Indiana, in which he writes policies for factories, stores, mills, dwellings, etc. He represents the well known Union Central Life Insurance Co. of Cincinnati, and writes accident policies for the Standard of Detroit. Mr. McKay is a director in the Commercial Club, owns considerable real estate here, and his success, liberality and public spirit is too well known to need further comment.

HERMAN KNIRIHM, NO. 33, E. MARKET ST.

INSURANCE AND STEAMSHIP AGENT.

The insurance business is peculiar in many respects, and one important feature is that the busy business man has not always the time or means at hand to examine into the merits or reliability of the different companies. He can and should fully know the reputation and candor of the local agent, and when satisfied that he is dealing with an agency that would not countenance unreliable ventures, he has only to indicate the amount of insurance which he desires to carry and the trustworthy agent will look after every other detail, as it is to his interest to protect his customer as well as to secure his company against unnatural loss.

Herman Knirihm is a native of Germany, residing in New Albany since 1854, and in the insurance business for nearly 20 years. He is the authorized agent for eleven well known companies. These companies represent many millions of dollars, and Mr. Knirihm can safely handle the largest risks. His customers have only to indicate their desires and every minutia is cared for. Mr. Knirihm is also agent for the North German Lloyd Steamship Co., and for the Netherlands line of steamships.

M. D. CONDIFF'S INSURANCE AGENCY.

CORNER BANK AND MAIN STREETS.

M. D. Condiff is a native of Bedford, Ind., read medicine and sold drugs in early manhood. He moved to New Albany in 1855, was engaged in the furniture trade here, and in the late war served for a time in the quarter master's department. Mr. Condiff engaged in the insurance business 24 years ago, since which his entire attention has been given to that line. He is agent for the Aetna and Hartford, of Hartford, Conn.; the Franklin, of Philadelphia, and other leading companies, covering fire, cargo, life, general accident, plate glass, employer's liability, boiler explosion, etc. Mr. Condiff is a notary public, and executes all descriptions of writings, requiring the notarial seal. He has been secretary of Jefferson lodge, F. & A. M., for 20 consecutive years.

R. E. BURK, REAL ESTATE AND INSURANCE.

NO. 9. EAST MAIN STREET.

Robert E. Burk is a native New Albanian, and commenced the insurance business thirteen years ago. He writes for the National, of Hartford; American, of Philadelphia; American, of New York; the New Hampshire, London Assurance, and Michigan Fire and Marine Insurance company, also the Travelers Life and Accident Co., of Hartford, Conn. Seven years ago he added real estate to his agency, and conducts a general business in that line. In company with others he owns a large interest in Silver hills plat, described elsewhere, is a director in the Highland electric raitway, and otherwise interested in the city's upbuilding.

MARSH & NEEDHAM, CORNER MARKET AND BANK.

INSURANCE AND REAL ESTATE AGENCY.

Frank Marsh is a native of New Albany, formerly assistant superintendent in the Ohio Falls Iron Works, and Dr. H. J. Needham was born in Louisville, graduated from the Pulte Medical College of Cincinnati, and for 12 years past has been engaged in the drug trade and practice of medicine here. In Feb, 1891, the above firm was formed to operate insurance, real estate and building and loan matters. The firm represents the Prussian National and Hamburg-Bremen, of Germany; the Imperial, of London; London-Lancashire, of Liverpool and Traders of Chicago, all solid companies. The above gentlemen are familliar with real estate values here, and their opening year has brought the success of industry, Their connection in building and loan matters will be mentioned under that interest.

RIDLEY & KLOSSE, REAL ESTATE AND INSURANCE.

OPPOSITE P. O. AT NO. 16, SPRING ST.

C. D. Ridley, a native of Brandenburg, Ky., who had been in Government work, in the west, purchased the real estate business of A. Huncilman, in 1886, subsequently adding insurance to his agency. In 1891, Henry F. Klosse, who had formerly been in the printing business, became a partner with Mr. Ridley. The firm represent a number of fire insurance companies, write accident policies, and conduct a general real estate agency, which has become a leading feature in their business. Some ex-

tensive sales have recently been negotiated by Messrs. Ridley & Klosse, while the
push and business tact of this comparatively new firm have brought them an encouraging success.

N. D. MORRIS—INSURANCE AND REAL ESTATE.
34, EAST SPRING STREET.

For nearly ten years, N. D. Morris served as assistant P. M., and five years ago
opened a real estate office as above. Mr. Morris is a native of New Albany and
thoroughly acquainted here. He represents several reliable insurance' companies
and transacts a general real estate business. He is secretary of the Howard Park
B. & L. association, and agent for the Mechanics.

A. W. BENTLY—INSURANCE.
NO. 3, EAST MAIN STREET.

Doubtless the oldest man in active business life, in New Albany, is Alfred W.
Bently, who was born in the state of New York, Oct. 20, 1809, and located in New
Albany in 1850. He took charge of the insurance business formerly conducted by
Elisha Sabin, in 1868, having since continued in the business. Mr. Bently's well
known philanthropy in Sunday school, church and lodge work has made him many
friends.

J. O. GREENE, 131, STATE SRTEET.
OWNER AND DEALER IN REAL ESTATE.

A native of Harrison county, John O. Greene has resided in this vicinity since 1858.
He owns about 60 acres, extending from Cherry street over the bluff to Oakwood,
and is principally interested in this street. Mr. Green is also a counselling attorney
and notary.

G. H. PADGETT, REAL ESTATE AND INRURANCE.
NO. 42, EAST SPRING STREET.

George H. Padgett was born in Lawrenceburg, in this state, and has resided in
New Albany since 1879. Cabinet work carpentering and contracting was his occupation, until receiving an injury last fall, when he retired from a successful business,
having built 17 houses in 1891. In April last he commenced in real estate, and already has a nice line of diversified property in his hands. He rents, collects and
looks after all branches of the business, also writing fire insurance risks in good companies. Mr. Padgett's office is with U. S. building and loan association at No. 42,
E. Spring.

OTHER ADDITIONS AND SURROUNDINGS.

Midway between the bridges, which cross the Ohio river here, and in the triangle
formed by Louisville, New Albany and Jeffersonville, on a plateau well above high
water mark, is found the thriving new village of Howard Park. The junction depot
is at this place, so that residents can go to either of the Falls cities every half hour,
and have good accomodation for freights. This village has recently been annexed to
the old incorporation of Clarksville, which was located by Gen. Geo. Rogers Clark,
before the beginning of the present century. Howard Park is principally owned by
Stotsenburg & Son, N. T. DePauw and others, who will give easy terms to purchasers.

Silver Grove lies just outside of the city limits, on the east side, and has recent-y become an incorporated village. This property was put on the market by Mayor McDonald several years ago, and Silver Grove is New Albany's most important suburban village. Lots not yet sold to purchasers are the property of the McDonald family, and can be secured on easy terms.

The Meadows, and place formerly occupied by Dr. Newland, near the city lim-ts, on State street, are owned by Geo. B. Cardwill, E. G. Henry, C. J. Frederick and J. W. Dunbar. The Meadows is very conveniently located, was easily sold, has been mostly taken, and is largely settled up. The Dr. Newland farm is now ready for development.

Glenview Park is a handsome suburban plat, 3 miles from Main street, and now in the hands of a syndicate. It will be accessible by the proposed Glenview Park railway, and will doubtless become desirable property.

GENERAL SUMMARY AND REVIEW.
READ THIS IF NOTHING MORE.

As some of our readers may not have time to peruse this entire sketch, we will briefly summarize for their benefit. Although articles may be found in this book which appear irrelevant to the text, (that of demonstrating to the world the superior advantages possessed by this city for diversified manufacturing) yet nearly every page brings out an important fact or convincing argument. We do not claim for this place a *big boom*, but steady and rapid increase for fifty years past, (see pages 13, 14.) The location of the place was well selected, and while the water power which should have been developed, pages 65-6, has not yet been realized, our facilities for obtaining cheap coal by river and rail, and iron working concerns for fitting manu-factories, 49-53, with other prominent facilities for obtaining raw materials, have re-sulted in the building up of a large manufacturing interest, see 45 to 62. There are 25 or more establishments in New Albany, which by reason of the magnitude of their operations, are contributing, in a marked degree, to the city's welfare. Several of these will be noted in subsequent pages, from which, at this writing, we have not yet received the historic facts. Extensive manufacturing give an impress of permanency, obtainable in no other way. New Albany has builded well, and has a grand foun-dation for extensive development in industrial enterprise. Located in the center of the magnificent Ohio Valley, at the head of deep water navigation, the New Albany wharfs can be easily and cheaply reached, from all rivers flowing into the great Father of Waters. By means of her exceptional railroad connections, 67-72, she can reach the markets of the country, and the principal cities, with great alacrity. Four rail-roads centering here, reach directly to St. Lous and the west, Chicago and the north-west, Indianapolis and the north, Cincinnati and the east, while the K. & I. Bridge Co., and Penn. lines give us immediate connection with Louisville and the trunk lines of the south. Our transportation facilities, cheap fuel, cheap living, that enables mechanics and laborers to work at reasonable rates, easy methods to secure homes, healthfulness and mild climate, all add to our advantages for successful progression. The product of a large iron furnace would be consumed in the Falls cities and there are many reasons why one would succeed here if judiciously managed. Agricultural implements, or any kind of iron working industry; furniture, carriage works, or other wood working factories; and many other lines of industry have as good or better chance of success here, than in most other sections of the country. With numerous real estate agents, many of whom are owners as well as agents; all realizing that extensive manufacturing gives solidity to a city which can be obtained in no other way, it is scarcely possible for speculative prices to be held against development. It is hardly necessary for us to refer again to the superior benevolent, financial, religious and educational facilities presented here, pages 20 to 40. Banking capital and surplus of over a million dollars, average deposits of as much more; two daily and six weekly papers, twenty churches, representing the leading denominations and holding property worth nearly half a million; a $30,000 Young Men's Christian Association now building; twelve public school buildings, and a $30,000 new structure going up; large catholic schools; DePauw College and New Albany Business College, all assist in the permanency, culture and success of the city.

We have superb water works and ample fire protection, pages 15, 42-3, which affords cheap insurance. Our hotel accommodation is but moderate, and a first class hostlery, with modern accommodations throughout, for travelers, has been in contemplation. A tourist hotel, at popular prices, or hygenic home, if in the hands of a live company and good manager, could be made to pay heavy returns. The climate here is void of either extreme, and a resort of this kind, could be run the year round. Louisville people, or those from the south, would enjoy the breezes of the highlands, and coolness of the parks, in the hottest summer weather; while persons. from the colder regions, of our northern latitude, would find that the most severe winter weather, of this section, was no great burden to them; as our cold season lasts but a few weeks at most. This suggestion is worth more than a passing thought, as by our Highland and Glenview Park railroads, the location would be in easy range of all the luxuries, amusements, etcetera, of the great metropolis across the river, and yet be entirely free from dust, smoke and city environments; in pure air, and with mineral springs of reputed value at our command. The Briggs mineral water, does not precipitate by standing, has been tested for many years in bowel, kidney, and other troubles, with abundant proof of efficiency, and could be kept in such a resort, at all times for use of guests. Several capitalists here, have expressed their willingness to take stock in a company for this proposed enterprise, and the proper person can easily secure needed encouragement, for erection of the Highland Hotel, or Glenview Hygienic Home. Who will make a move for this needed development?

We have several brick yards in the outskirts of the city, and with unexcelled clay for vitrified brick. a large industry should be built up in this direction. The shale on some of the surrounding farms has been tested for the production of pressed brick and the specimens produced have no superiors. Excellent cement rock is abundant in this section, and with superb dressing stone in the near by quarries there is no lack of material for fine architectural development.

With the immense quantities of leather produced here, the cheapness of labor and living, this is just the place for starting a large harness manufactory. We have a few small concerns; but nothing calculated to meet the wholesale trade, and there is no better place in the country for a large establishment in that line than right here. East Liverpool, Ohio, with one railroad and the river, has built up an immense pottery interest. The clay for queensware, stoneware, tiling, etc., must be selected and shipped from various sections of the country, and as we have excellent transportation facilities, with near by markets, there is abundance of reason why large potteries in good hands could be made an unqualified success in New Albany.

Floyd and adjoining counties on the Ohio, present some magnificent tracts for peaches, pears, apples, etc. The peach crop is a special favorite in many places, and when the location is well selected, the crop is rarely destroyed by frosts, and proves very remunerative. Our townsmen, J. H. Stotsenburg & Sons, have 1200 acres of peach lands, some 25 miles above this place in Clark county. About 75,000 peach trees, and a large variety of plums, apples, quinces and cherries are found in their orchards. An incline is used for sending the crates from the bluffs to the boat landing and other labor saving devices for marketing the products.

Agriculturally the city is in the centre of the small fruit culture of the Ohio valley. Strawberries, raspberries, blackberries, cherries, grapes, peaches and apples are raised in marvellous abundance almost within the city limits, and many hundred of thousands of crates are shipped each year to her easily reached markets. As a place of residence, New Albany has few equals. Her population of 25,000 people, walk and ride through many miles of paved streets, lined with handsome residences, and universally shaded with beautiful trees. At the western border of the city runs a range of exceedingly picturesque hills, reached by an electric railway, and rapidly filling up with comfortable homes overlooking the Ohio winding so gracefully below.

In area, New Albany covers nine square miles, and recent suburban additions will add perhaps another mile to this. The real estate valuation, with outside property, which is practically a part of the city, will not fall short of $20,000,000. With two electric light companies, and gas works, we have competitive illumination, and small manufactories are easily and cheaply run by water or electric motors. Our mercantile pages will show that, while we are under the shadow of Louisville, we are represented by progressive merchants abreast of the times.

New Albany is thus seen to be full of solid advantages. Surrounded by beautiful scenery, offering every attraction to those desiring rest and recreation, and by steamboat. railroad, electric car and street car, in a brief time and trifling expense, these garden spots of pure air and charming views may be reached. Handsome stores and elegant public buildings, abound here. Conspicuous among the latter may be mentioned the fine stone courthouse, and the imposing United States custom house and postoffice. Free postal delivery is to be enumerated among the conveniences we enjoy, and we occupy our homes in peace and security under the care of one of the most competent fire departments in the country. In fact, any man who has the stamina to go west or south with limited means, trusting to his energy and the smiles of Providence, has greater certainty of success right here. He finds in the Ohio valley no devastating grasshoppers, nor blasting drouths. His products are near the great markets, and his necessities are easily and cheaply supplied. If the illustrious Horace Greeley was here at present, instead of saying "young man, go west," he would doubtless second our efforts by saying, "stay at home and do your best."

MEDICAL AND LEGAL PROFESSIONS.

By some it may be claimed that in describing the essential features of a city, " professional notes " are a matter of minor importance, and the space might better have been occupied with statistics or valuable data. It is not only difficult, but impossible, to meet the requirements of all, and while we shall attempt to please the majority, our experience has taught us that people take pleasure in mailing to distant friends a pamphlet containing the name and business mention of their personal acquaintances; conseqently these notes, while seemingly unimportant, assist us in securing that wide-spread distribution which is so essential in making this production valuable to New Albany, and to all advertisers. The ease of wrapping and inexpensiveness of mailing this pamphlet to friends, its convenient shape for preservation, together with the fact that all subscribers for the pamphlet have agreed to make judicious distribution of the same, justify us in asserting that this sketch will have a more judicious circulation than any other descriptive sketch of a similar character which has been issued from this city.

Probably no river city in the west has made a better record for healthfulness than New Albany. There is no stagnant water nor malarial surroundings here. The drainage is naturally easy and with a sewerage system perfected the sanitary condition will be of the best. Yet accidents will happen, chronic and epidemic diseases arise, ignorant and more intelligent people transgress the laws of nature, and the city has its full quota of physicians, surgeons, dentists and vetenary doctors.

The first permanent physician of New Albany was Dr. Asahel Clapp, who located here in 1817. He identified himself with the material interests of the place, was prominently connected in the progress of New Albany, and built up a large practice, on which he was engaged until his death in 1862.

Dr. William A. Clapp, son of the above, was born in this city, Oct. 29, 1822; educated in the private schools, conducted by Prof. Sturdevant and Prof. Spence, after which he read medicine in his father's office, and graduated from the Jefferson Medical College of Philadelphia in 1848. He at once commenced practice in this city with his father, and excepting his time of service as surgeon of the 38th, Ind., Reg., in the late war, he has been in continuous practice here for 44 years. It is rather a remarkable fact that Dr. Clapp's life has practically been spent in one place, his office and residence having always remained at the place of his birth, No. 11, East Main street.

Dr. John Sloan, was born in Maine, Sept. 25, 1815, graduated at Bowdoin Medical College, in his native state, in 1838, and located in New Albany, the same year. He had charge of a hospital here, as contract surgeon, during the late war. When he commenced in New Albany, Drs. Leonard, Dowling, Shields, Cooper, and eight or ten others, were in practice, all now gone. Many others have come and gone within the 54 years in which he has been in continuous practice here. Dr. Sloan has been prominently connected in the regular medical societies, county, state and national, but never sought for political preference. His office and residence is 157, E. Main street.

Dr. Seymour C. Wilcox, was born in N. Y., Sept. 20, 1818, graduated from the Geneva Medical College in 1841, having now been in practice for more than half a century. He located in New Albany 24 years ago, and has since been identified with this city. Dr. Wilcox is president of the Cemetery board of regents. His office and residence is at No. 273, E. Spring street.

Dr. John L. Stewart is a native of Switzerland county, attended the Vevay Academy, read medicines with Dr. W. C. Sweezy, in his native county; and graduated from the Kentucky School of Medicine, in 1865. He served in the late war, a portion of the time being in hospital work. Dr. Stewart engaged in the drug trade of New Albany, with John R. Sigmon, in 1868, continuing for 10 years, since which his entire time has been given to medical practice. Office at No. 149, State street.

Dr. Geo. H. Cannon is a native of this city; after the public schools attended Forest Home Academy, in Ky., and returning to New Albany took a course at Prof. W. W. May's *Eikosi*. Dr. Cannon graduated from the medical department of the University of Louisville, in March, 1877, at once locating in practice here. He is a member of the state and county medical societies and physician to the United Charities Hospital. The doctor occupies nicely furnished rooms at 114, E. Main street.

Dr. E. P. Easley is a native of Kentucky, attended the Seminary of Orleans, Ind., graduated from the medical department of the University of Louisville, in 1872, and located in New Albany, where he has been in practice for 20 years. Office and residence 175, E. Spring street.

Dr. J. H. Lemon is a native of Bloomington, Ind., educated at the State University, and the medical department of the Mich. University, locating here Jan. 1868. He served in detached duty as hospital stewart in 3d Div. 14th Army Corps. Dr. Lemon has been coroner, county physician, and is a present member of the city board of health.

Dr. H. S. Wolfe is a native of Floyd county, was educated in private schools, learned the shoemaker's trade which he followed for some time, graduated from the Kentucky School of Medicine in 1860, and commenced practice at Washington, Ind. Seven years later he received the degree of M. D., from the Kentucky University, after which he located at Corydon. In 1886 he removed to New Albany. Dr. Wolfe was surgeon of the 81st Ind., Reg., 1862-3. He owns a farm of 216 acres near Georgetown, makes a specialty of breeding fine sheep and swine, and spends much of his time in agricultural pursuits. Dr. Wolfe is an active democrat, but has usually declined political preferment.

Dr. E. L. Sigmon was born in this city, educated in the High school, read medicine with Dr. J. L. Steward, and graduated from the Kentucky School of Medicine in 1886. Dr. Sigmon has made a special study of surgery, and for one so young, has made a prominent start in this direction. His office is with Dr. Steward at 149, State street.

Dr. C. W. McIntyre first saw the light on the Emerald Isle, was brought to America in childhood, read medicine and graduated from the McGill University, of Montreal. Canada, in 1864. He practiced for some years in Jefferson county. Ind., and in 1873, took the addendum course, and graduated from the University of Louisville. Dr. McIntyre has, for 12 years past, been practicing in New Albany, office and residence, 150, Vincennes street. He is a member of the Floyd Co. and Am. Medical societies.

Dr. C. W. McIntyre, Jr., son of the above, is a native of Jefferson county, a graduate of New Albany High school, and in 1887, received a diploma from the University, of Louisville. His office is over Klossce's old drug store stand, on State street.

Dr. J. N. Payne was born in Mercer county, Ky., and after an academical course, took the A. B. degree from the Kentucky Military Institute, of Frankfort, teaching for many years in New Albany and elsewhere. Later he read medicine, and a few years since graduated from the Louisville University. Since which he has been in practice in this city. Dr. Payne is president of the Floyd Co. Medical Society, and secretary of the county board of health. No. 402, E. Spring street.

Dr. Frank H. Wilcox is a native of this city, graduated from the N. A. Business College. 1886, read medicine in his father's office, and graduated from the University of Louisville. Mar. 1890, having since been in practice here. He is a member of the city board of health, and vice president of the Floyd Co. Medical Society.

Dr. Chas. P. Cook, a native of this county, attended Prof. Pinkham's school at Paoli, and graduated from the teacher's department of the Ladoga Normal school. In 1883, he took the degree of M. D. from the medical department of the University of Louisville, having since been in practice here. Dr. Cook is surgeon for the Air Line and K. & I. Bridge Co. He is a member of the American and local medical societies. He is largely interested in city real estate.

Dr. Dumont Garey, a native of Harrison county, attended the High school of Corydon, read medicine with Dr. J. E. Lawson of that place, and in 1889 graduated from the University of Louisville, having since been in practice here. Dr. Garey owns a well fitted drug store, at the corner of Elm and Vincennes streets, with residence and office on opposite corners.

Dr. B. Buest, from a noted Prussian family, graduated in medicine at Leipsic, Germany; came to America 1852; served as brigade surgeon in 9th army corps, in the war, and subsequently located in this city where he has since been in practice and drug trade, at 330, E. Market st.

Dr. M. Buest, son of the above, was born in Philadelphia, finished his literary course at Morse's Academy, graduated from the Louisville College of Pharmacy, in 1874, and in 1881, from the Hospital College of Medicine, of Louisville. His office and residence is 290, Vincennes street.

Dr. Geo. U. Runcie graduated from the Chicago Medical College, in 1880, and practiced medicine at Fort Branch, this state, until July 1889, when having been elected as physician to the state prison at Jeffersonville, he located in New Albany. Dr. Runcie received a diploma from the University of Louisville in 1890. His office and residence is at 207, E. Elm street., and as he has competent assistants in the prison, he finds opportunity for general practice in New Albany.

Dr. F. A. Mitchell, a native of Ohio, attended lectures at the University of Louisville, 1859-60, practiced at New Providence, for a time, graduating from the above school in 1865. He was several years in the wholesale drug trade with O. Sackett, practiced in Perry county for 15 years, in the mean time taking a post graduate course at the University of Louisville, and Jan. 92 returned to New Albany, where he is making a specialty of the treatment of nasal catarrh, throat and ear diseases, which has been his practice for 9 years.

Dr. R. W. Harris was born in Mt. Washington, Ky., and after an academic education, graduated from the Hospital College of Medicine at Louisville, in 1883. Dr. Harris practiced three years in his native town, and 4 years in Kansas prior to locating in New Albany, Jan. 1, 1890. His office is at corner Oak and Vincennes sts.

Dr. A. P. Hauss, a native of Cincinnati, attended the graded schools of Liberty,

Ind., and graduated from the Eclectic Medical Institute of Cincinnati, in 1879. He practiced in Clark Co. for 8 years, locating here in 1887. Dr. Hauss belongs to the Association of Railway Surgeons, and is surgeon to the J., M. & I. R. R. He is a member of the National Eclectic Assocnation, and is first vice president of the Indiana Eclectic Medical Association. Office 338, E. Market; residence adjoining.

Dr. G. O. Erni, is a native of this state, graduated from the Louisville Medical College in 1882, and has been in practice in New Albany since 1885. He is a member of the city board of health, and physician to the Old Ladies Home. Dr. Erni has a convenient office at 214, Spring street, corner of East Eighth.

Dr. L. D. Levi is a native of Harrison Co., attended Prof. Jas. G. May's Academy at Salem, Ind., and graduated from the Louisville Medical College, in 1879. He practiced at Georgetown, this county, for 10 years, graduating, in 1890, from the New York Homoeopathic Medical College, where he also attended the Polyclinic. For 2 years past, Dr. Levi's office has been at No. 40, E. Spring street.

Dr. E. A. Severinghaus, a native of Ohio, graduated from the Seymour High school, in 1886, and from the Louisville Medical College in 1890. He then graduated from the Hahneman Medical College, Philadelphia, the following year locating in New Albany. His office is 92½, E. Market street.

DENTISTS AND DRUGGISTS.

Dr. P. T. Greene, is a native of Harrison Co., and has been in the practice of dentistry since 1860. After practicing four years in the West, he located here in 1864. Several years since accepting his son as a partner. The office is at No. 103, Bank street.

Dr. Frank C. Greene is a native of Iowa, and 20 years ago began the practice of dentistry with his father. He graduated from the Western College of Dental Surgeons at St. Louis in 1880. He has convenient rooms and a well fitted office with his father.

Dr. Theo. B. Buest, was born in New Albany, attended our city High school, graduated from the Hospital College of Medicine, and the Louisville College of Dentistry, in 1889. He took a post graduate course in crown and bridge work, locating on the corner of Spring and Bank, in the fall of 89. Dr. Buest has a complete dental outfit.

Dr. J. B. Harrison, a New Albanian, graduated from the High school class of 84, attended DePauw University 2 years, practiced dentistry with Dr. F. C. Greene, graduating from the Missouri Dental College of St. Louis, in 1891. He has convenient office rooms at No. 42, E. Spring street.

Dr. C. L. Hoover & Sons conduct an extensive Drug house, which was established by the senior partner 40 years ago, and there are 25 retail stores in that line. Some large stores, on main streets, and away from the principal business street, we find standard houses.

Jos. L. Stacy, successor to Brashear & Crosier, among enterprising side druggists, keeps a good line of drugs, and a fine stock of perfumes, brushes and toilet articles, corner of Oak and E. Eighth streets.   '

Ollie Owens way out on Vincennes street, opposite the woolen mills, has a well assorted stock, and does an etensive business.

LEGAL PROFESSION.—Among the early attorneys, in New Albany, R. W. Nelson, who was also editor of the Cresent, came about 1824; Lathrop Elderkin, came about 1825; H. H. Moore, in 26; Randall Crawford, 28; Henry Collins, 30; James Collins, 33; Maj. H. Thornton, J. S. Davis, T. J. Barnett, Groves & Griswald, 36; W. M. Dunn, 38; T. L. Smith, 39; P. M. Kent, 41; Jas. C. Moody, 42; A. P. Willard, 44; W. T. Otto and M. C. Kerr, 48; Geo. V. Howk, 49; Geo. A. Bicknell, 51; R. M. Weir, Brown and Stotsenburg, in 54.

John H. Stotsenburg was born in Wilmington, Delaware, and graduated from Trinity College, Hartford Connecticut; read law with Chief Justice Gilpin, and was admitted to practice in 1853. The next year he located here, becoming a partner with Thos. M. Brown. This partnership continued until the death of Mr. Brown, in 1871. Mr. Stotsenburg served as city attorney 1856-9, and was elected in the fall of 1860 to the general assembly, which gained the title of the "War Legislature." He was on the commission to revise the Indiana code of laws, and as a legal adviser, has gained a wide reputation. He was one of the incorporators of the K. & I. Bridge Co., and the Belt & Terminal railroad, and has been variously interested in New Albany's success. For several years past Mr. Stotsenburg has been largely interested in fruit growing. Recently he has retired from practice and will hereafter devote his principal attention to fruit culture.

Evan B. Stotsenburg, is a native of this city, and after a course at the High school, attended Kenyon college, and took a special course at the New Albany Business college. He read law with his father, was admitted to the bar, May 17, 1886, since which he has been in practice here. Mr. Stotsenburg is lecturer on Commercial law at the N. A. Business college; county attorney for 1890-3, is secretary of the new Glenview Park Railway, and is abreast of the times in business matters. Office No. 9, E. Main street.

Alex. Dowling is a native of Va., but was brought to this city in infancy. He was educated at Anderson's Collegiate Institute, read law with Otto & Davis, and was admitted to practice in 1858. Mr. Dowling served as district attorney for two years, city attorney for eight years, and has been a leading corporation and railroad lawyer for many years. He occupies commodious and well fitted offices over New Albany Banking Company, and is largely interested in the manufacturing and financial concerns of this place.

James V. Kelso, (son of the late J. D. Kelso, who commenced the practice of law here in 1854,) is a native of Madison, attended Asbury University of Greencastle, taught four years as principal of the Spring street school, read law with his father and John M. Wilson, and was admitted to practice in 1860. In the late war he served as quartermaster of the 38th Ind., and in 65 located permanently in practice here. Mr. Kelso served 10 years as county attorney, 8 years as city attorney, and was editor on the Standard and Ledger-Standard for some time. With 27 years in practice he has secured a large clientage.

Chas. D. Kelso, son of the above, is a native New Albanian, attended the city High school, graduated from the N. A. Business college, and in 1883, from the law department of the Louisville University, since which time he has been a partner in practice with his father. He served as city attorney 1885-9. Office of Kelso & Kelso at No 7, E. Main.

W. W. Tuley, born in this city in 1827, served in the Mexican war, was clerk in the state legislature for 5 years, city clerk 5 years, county clerk 8 years, 7 years on the school board, and in 1883, was the Floyd county representative to the state legislature. Colonel Tuley was admitted to the bar In 1869, for 7 years was a partner with Judge Howk, 11 years with Judge LaFollette, and is the senior partner of the firm of Tuley & Herter. He has served as administrator on a very large number of estates, and as guardian to many children in this county. He is secretary and treasurer of the Highland Railway.

Jacob Herter, was born in Germany, in 1842, and was brought to Harrison Co., Ind., in 1846. He read law with Smith & Kerr, and was admitted to the bar in 1864, served as city judge for a year, city attorney for 2 years, and was appointed, by the county officials, to fill the vacancy occasioned by the death of the late Judge Howk, officiating until Judge Cardwill was appointed by the Governor.

Thos. L. Smith, born in this city, read law with Smith & Kerr, and was admitted to the bar in 1869. He was elected criminal judge in 72, serving until that office was abolished, subsequent to which he was prosecuting attorney for a term. Office, 142, Pearl street.

E. G. Henry was born in Switzerland county, graduated from the law department of the University at Bloomigton, Ind., in 1872, and located in New Albany where he has been in continuous practice for 20 years. Mr. Henry is a director in the Commercial Club, is a partner in several plats in or near the city, and has shown a deep interest in New Albany's improvement. He occupies a well fitted office at No. 29, E. Main, corner of Pearl. He served in the Legislature of 1888-9.

Wm. C. Utz, is a native of this county, attended the state Normal school at Bloomington, Ill, for 2 years, read law with Chas. L. Jewett, and was admitted May 12, 1886. He was elected prosecuting attorney for the 52d Judicial district, Nov. 1890, for a two years term. Office rooms, 6 and 7, Masonic building.

Wm. D. Marshall was reared in Seymour, Ind., graduated from Hanover college, in 1885, read law with his father, and was admitted to the bar of Jackson county, in 1887. After two years practice in that county he located in New Albany, and holds a convenient office on the corner of State and Market streets.

Geo. B. McIntyre was reared in Indiana, graduated from the city High school class of 87, read law with C. L. & H. E. Jewett, graduated in law, at Ann Arbor, Mich:, 1891; since which he has been in practice here. Mr. McIntyre was nominated for assemblyman, from this county, at the democratic primaries, and this district being largely Democratic, he will probably represent Floyd, after the Nov. election. Office rooms, 8 and 9, Masonic building.

G. H. Hester is a native of New Albany, graduated from the High school, May 1888, read law with J. H. Stotsenburg, and graduated from the law department of the Michigan University, June 24, 1891. He has a commission as Notary and executes writings, requiring a notarial seal. Office, corner Pearl and Market streets, over New Albany Banking Company.

J. K. Marsh is a native of Harrison county, was admitted to the bar in 1867, and has been in continuous practice in Clark Co. for 25 years. He served as prosecuting attorney for 6 years, and was a member of the state legislature in 1877-8.

E. D. Mitchell, also a native of Harrison Co., recently graduated from the law department of the University of Louisville, and in company with Mr. Marsh has opened an office at rooms No. 16 & 17, Masonic building.

The prosecuting attorneys who were residents of this city, since 1850, have been M. C. Kerr, in 52; R. M. Weir, 54, again in 66–8; Thos. M. Brown, 56–64; D. W. LaFollette, 70; R. J. Shaw, 72; T. L. Smith, 78, and Wm. C. Utz, elected 1890.

The district attorneys, until the abolishment of the Common Please Court, were Willett Bullitt, 1856; Jas. A. Ghormley, 60; T. J. Jackson, 67, and R. G. Shaw, 68.

Lawrence B. Huckeby is a native of Perry county, Ind., and has resided in this city for 22 years. He learned the blacksmith trade, served for some years as a teacher, read law and was admitted in 1870, going into practice with his brother. In 1877 he was appointed a justice of the peace, and has continuously held that office ever since. His rooms are at 98 State street.

John J. Richards is a native of this city, served as mayor 1883–9, was appointed as justice in 89, and elected in 90, for a term of four years.

The U. S. Boiler Inspector, for the 6th supervising district, is G. E. Riggle, a native of this city, who has been a machinist and marine engineer for 30 years past.

SOCIAL SOCIETIES, ASSOCIATIONS, ETC.

While the educational and religious features of a place have due weight with the intelligent prospective settler, the secret societies, or other social attractions, are a matter to which much importance is attached by some persons, and we shall herewith show some of New Albany's advantages from a social and moral aspect.

The Crusaders, or Knight of the Temple, which were organized in 1096 with the avowed intent of wresting Jerusalem and the Holy Land from the hands of the Turks, was the earliest modern secret society of which we have authentic record. This organization assumed a military character and many thousands of lives were sacrificed in what was considered to be a religious cause.

ANCIENT FREE AND ACCEPTED MASONS.

Free Masons has its rites and ceremonies founded upon the traditions of the building of King Solomon's Temple, and some of its devotees claim for it a continued existence among skilled operative Masons from that time to the present date, but its origin may be said to have been lost in remote antiquity. It is undoubtedly an ancient and respectable institution, embracing among its members men of every rank and condition of life, and stands prominent among the institutions established for the improvement of mankind It is said that ancient Master Masons met at York, A. D., 926, and at least one Scottish lodge has written records extending back to 1599. Elias Ashmole in 1664 gave in his diary an account of his initiation into the society. Twenty years later after the great London fire, Sir Christopher Wren, then grand master of the order in that city, secured prompt financial aid for the suffering Masons, and the society flourished, accepting from time to time princes, potentates and rulers, as honorary members, who had not been proficient in operative work. In 1702 St. Paul's lodge, of London, then the only active Masonic lodge in existence, dropped the operative restriction and agreed to accept as a candidate any man, free born, of mature age, moral character, sound body, and under the tongue of good Masonic report. In 1717, four lodges united to form the Grand Lodge of England, and from this the advent of speculative Free Masonry may properly be dated. It soon spread to France and other countries of the continent, and in 1733 was introduced in America. Washington organized and conducted American Union Lodge,

No. 1, in the Colonial army. At present there is no country on the civilized globe in which it has not gained a foothold, and its membership exceeds 3,000,000, numbering in its ranks many of the most celebrated men of the age, covering all shades of religious and political belief.

Masonry was early introduced into New Albany, Zif lodge, No. 8, having been started Aug. 11, 1819; Dr. Asahel Clapp, W. M.; Chas. Paxson, S. W.; Lathrop Elderkin, J. W. This lodge suspended in 1828.

New Albany, No. 39, was organized Sep. 1833. The present membership is 121. Wm. A. Laufer, W. M.; H. M. Huckeby, S. W.; J. L. Stacy, J. W.; G. A. Newhouse, Treas.; L. B. Huckeby, Sec. Meets 1st and 3d Thursdays.

Jefferson, No. 104, was started Nov. 7, 1849. The present membership is over 120. Meetings are held 2d and 4th Thursdays. J. R. Morris, W. M.; C. S. Mebane, S. W.; W. E. Stoy, J. W.; W. F. Tuley, Treas.; M. D. Condiff, Sec.

DePauw, No. 338, organized May 29, 1867, has about 100 members. J. M. Boyd, W. M.; Geo. F. Goodbub, S. W.; Wm. Arnold, J. W.; W. L. Smith, Treas.; G. W. Harrison Sec. Meets 2d and 4th Tuesdays.

Pythagoras No. 355, German, was organized in 1857. and has over 30 members. Meets 1st and 3d Tuesdays. Adam Heimberger, W. M.; Herman Rockenbach, Sec.

Royal Arch Chapter, No. 17, was organized July 8th, 1850, and has 125 companions. Geo. A. Newhouse, sr., H. P.; John R. Morris, jr., King; Wm. P. Decker, Scribe; M. D. Condiff, Sec. Convocations 1st Monday of each month.

N. A. Commandery, No. 5, of Knights Templar, was organized Sept. 22, 1854, and has 125 Sir Knights. Communications are held on 4th Mondays. Eugene W. Walker, E. C.; John J. Richards, Gen.; W. C. Nunemacher, C. G.; M. D. Condiff, Rec.

Indiana Council, No. 1, Royal and Select Masters, chartered Sept. 4th, 1854, has about 80 members. Stated convocations 2d Monday of April, July, Oct. and Dec. W. C. Nunemacher, I. M.; Wm. Briggs, Treas.; M. D. Condiff, Rec.

All the masonic bodies meet in the elegant halls of Masonic building, corner Pearl and Spring streets.

Colored masons claim to work under dispensation from the Grand Lodge of England.

INDEPENDENT ORDER OF ODD FELLOWS.

A society of the Ancient and Honorable Loyal Odd Fellows was formed about the beginning of the present century, and from its fantastic and convivial character was probably originated as a burlesque on the Free. Masons, but in 1812, some of the brotherhood at Manchester, England, conceived the plan for the continuance of the order on noble and lasting principles—prompt attendance and disbursement of funds to a sick brother, administrations to the needs of the widows and education of the orphans—fellowship, love and truth. April 26, 1819, Thomas Wilder, of Manchester, and four others, organized the first lodge of the Independent Order of Odd Fellows in the United States at Baltimore, Md., naming it Washington Lodge, No. 1. Eleven months later a second lodge was located at Boston, and December 26, 1821, the third society was organized at Philadelphia. The Sovereign Grand Lodge of America was formed at Baltimore, June, 1823, and from that date the order made a rapid growth in the new world. There are some 50 grand lodges on this continent, with 6,500 subordinate lodges and a membership of over 600,000. The membership in Europe is approximately the same, aggregating about one and one-fourth millions of Odd Fellows.

Odd Fellowship, in Indiana, had its birth in New Albany, May 25th, 1835, but as stage coaches were slow in these early days, a charter was not received and lodge instituted until Feb. 3, 36. This was held in Drysdale block, cor. E. 3d and Main. New Albany Lodge, No. 1, had 9 charter members, grew slowly on account of dissensions; it suspended on Sept. 5, 41, and No. 10 was organized as its successor.

New Albany, No. 10—Organized May 31, 1841, has over 150 members. J.

E. Seigle, N. G.; W. A. Felger, V. G.; J. W. Buck, R. S.; W. M. Mix, P. S.; Edmond Caye, Treas. Meets every Thursday.

New Albany, No. 1.—In 1851, several members of the defunct No. 1, resolved upon reorganizing and securing a new charter under the old number, the present lodge was organized Aug. 13, 1851. The membership now is about 170. H. T. Gandy, N. G.; Jno. Sullivan, V. G.; J. G. Harrison, P. S.; G. Tufts, sr., R. S.; G. W. Harrison, Treas. Meets every Monday.

Hope Lodge, No. 83, was organized Feb. 23, 1850, and at present numbers about 265. G. M. Streepy, N. G.; Chas. Wright, V. G.; J. O. English, P. S.; G. P. Bornwasser, R. S.; D. N. Silberman, Treas. Meets every Friday. All the above lodges and encampment occupy the commodious hall at n. e. cor. Bank and Market, in common.

Humboldt, No. 234, German I. O. O. F., meets at n. e. cor. State and Market streets, every Wednesday. Present membership about 60. This lodge was organized Aug. 24, 1864. Gustav Naef, N. G.; Conrad Kraft, R. S.; Jacob Herter, P. S.

Jerusalem Encampment, No. 1, was first organized in 1836. After 5 years it lay dormant until 1848, since which it has continued in active work. The present membership is about 110. Meets 1st and 3d Tuesdays. G. M. Streepy, C. P.; S. S. Stalcup, Scribe.

New Albany Canton, No. 35, meets on 2d and 4th Tuesdays at Odd Fellows Hall. Thos. B. Love, Capt.; Jacob Best, Lieut.; T. L. Mullineaux, Acct.; W. L. Town, Clerk.

I. O. O. F. General Relief was organized Jan. 14, 1853, and has dispensed several thousands of dollars in charity. It is composed of 3 members from each lodge.

Collored G. U. O. F.—Edmonds Lodge, No. 1544, and St. Pauls Lodge, No. 1546, colored lodges, work under charters granted by the Grand United Odd Fellows of England.

IMPROVED ORDER OF RED MEN.

It is claimed that this order started in the days of the Revolution, but if so it lay dormant from that time until revived by Lieut. Williams, at Fort Mifflin, on the Delaware, in 1813. A few years later, shorn of its political character, it was propagated in different places, on principles of benevolence and fraternity. It has moved on a very quiet Quaker like plan, doing good and dispensing charity, and has a present membership of about 120,000.

Pawnee Tribe, No. 37, was organized Apl. 27, 1873, and has about 75 brothers. Wm. O'Conner, W. S.; Wm. Dermont, S. S.; Edw. Wolfe, J. S.; E. Thomas, sr., Pro.; E. Thomas, jr., C. of R.; H. Waters, K. of W. Meets Wednesdays, n. w. cor. Pearl and Market.

KNIGHTS OF PYTHIAS.

The order of Knights of Pythias was conceived from the play of "Damon and Pythias" by an actor, Justice H. Rathbone, of Washington, D. C., who organized the society Feb. 19, 1864. It is of a chivalric or semi-military character, teaching with striking force the principles of bravery, charity, humanity, benevolence and unselfish friendship. The order now has a membership considerably above 300,000.

Friendship, No. 10, was organized Sept. 1871, and has about 210 members at present. Adolph Goetz, C. C.; J. R. Morris, jr., K. of R. & S. Meets every Wednesday night.

Ivanhoe, No. 15, was organized soon after the above and has about 185 members. J. S. Malbon, C. C.; H. M. Cooper, K. of R. & S. Meets every Thursday night.

Rowena, No. 28, was organized April 25th, 1873, and also has about 185 members. Alex. Hall, C. C.; W. H. Ratcliff, K of R. & S. Meets every Friday. All above meet in K. P. Hall, at No. 85, State st. There is also a Uniform and Endowment rank connected with the above lodges.

GRAND ARMY OF THE REPUBLIC.

This organization was founded in 1866 in Illinois, and has a present membership of about 450,000. It is composed exclusively of men who served in the late war against the states which seceded from the Union, and is a patriotic organization designed to cherish the memories of the fallen comrades, assist and fraternize the living soldiers and dispense charities to the widows and orphans of the deceased. The order has probably reached its acme, as it has incorporated in its ranks the majority of those from the late war who are still living, and the death rate must now necessarily be about as large as the increase from those who are eligible that still remain outside its folds. Under the present constitutional requirements it can be but a few years at most until the order must succumb for the want of material, and the Sons of Veterans has been organized as a society to perpetuate the memories of the fathers.

W. L. Sanderson Post, 191, was organized June 28, 1883, with 30 charter members, now having about 175 comrades. Geo. H. Cook, P. C.; H. E. Koetter, Adj.; Chas. H. Sowle, Q. M. Meets every Friday night.

Robt. H. Sage Post, 581, Was organized Sept. 1890, and has a membership of about 40. John Jackson, P. C.; Leonard Leach, Adj.; Lucky Smith, Q. M. Post meets on Mondays. Hurst Circle of ladies works in connection with this and Sanderson Relief Corps with the other G. A. R. Post. All have rooms at s. w. corner Pearl and Market.

The Union Veteran Legion, was organized Mar. 1884, at Pittsburg. Pa., with the object in view of fraternizing the ex-soldiers who are justly entitled to the term veteran, by early enlistment and long service in the cause of the Union, unless discharged for proper causes while serving in the line of duty. The order now has encampments in about 20 states and the membership is rapidly increasing. Encampment, No. 101, was organized, in New Albany, Oct. 5, 1891. Louis Bir, who was recently elected as councilman from the 1st ward, is colonel, and C. H. Sowle, Adj.

ANCIENT ORDER OF UNITED WORKMEN.

The above order is the oldest of its kind in the United States, having been established at Meadville, Pa., October 28, 1868, and now having a membership of over 270,000, which is largely in excess of any other beneficiary organization. Prior to June 1, 1891, the A. O. U. W. had paid to the relatives of deceased members $35,-737,673, and is now carrying insurance risks aggregating $540,000,000. The full $2,000 has in all cases been promptly paid, without litigation, upon proper proofs of the death of any brother in good standing, and the order has a record of reliability not excelled by any beneficiary organization. It is not, as its name would seem to imply, a fraternity of workingmen, but strictly a mutual insurance and fraternal society composed of all phases of business, social and religious preferences.

Morning Star, No. 7, was organized July, 1873, and has a present membership of 115. It meets every Thursday night at the n. e. cor. State and Market. Edward Crumbo, W. M.; Theo. Park, Fin.; Matt. Klarer, Treas.; Jacob Herter, Rec.

KNIGHTS AND LADIES OF HONOR.

The Knights of Honor, similar in all respects to the A. O. U. W., was organized in 1873, and has a membership of about 140,000. The order has paid to beneficiaries more than thirty-five millions of dollars.

Oceola, No. 47, was established the first year of the order, and has over 150 members. Meets 2d and 4th Tuesdays. Wm. Michels, Dict.; Geo. Borgerding, F. R.; Conrad Kraft, Treas.; M. D. Condiff, Rep.

New Albany, No. 922, organized in 1879, has about 70 members. Meets 1st and 3d Tuesdays; J. A. Hucklebury, Dict.; J. L. Washburn, F. R.; Jos. Pratt, Treas.; J. O. Cavin, Rep.

The Knights and Ladies of Honor, the first fraternal society insuring women, upon a level basis with men, was organized at Louisville in 1876, and has a present membership of 72,000. Insurance ranges $500 to $3,000.

Goodwill, No. 17, was organized Feb. 11th, 1879, and has a membership of over 350, Linda Wiseman, Prot ; Susie Ried, V. P.; H. A. Rehling, Sec.; Geo. H. Godfrey, F. S.; J. M. Shaney, Treas. Meets every Thursday.

KNIGHTS OF LABOR.

Labor organizations in the various departments of industry have flourished from time to time; but no preconcerted action to unite all forms of labor under one grand banner was taken until about 10 years ago. The Knights of Labor organized for the above purpose, made a phenomenal growth, raising its membership in a few brief years, to several hundreds ot thousands.

Assembly, No. 3115, was organized in New Albany, Nov. 20, 1884, and has a present membership of about 70. It is the parent of several labor organizations here. All honorable toilers are eligible to membership. and as fast as any class has the required number of its craft, they are banded together as a separate body. This Assembly has a large library for the use of its members, and occupies Clapp's Hall, on Main st. Meetings 1st and 3d Thursdays in each month.

THE COMMERCIAL CLUB.—This society was organized Dec. 3, 1889, to promote the commercial interests and general welfare of the city of New Albany and vicinity. It has made a special effort to aid in manufacturing development, and advertise the advantages of this place. It has about 200 members, comprising many of the ablest business men of New Albany, and its officers will gladly furnish to prospective settlers. for manufacturing or residential purposes, any required information not found in these pages. A committee from the directors of the club has supervised these pages and endorse this pamphlet as correct in every essential feature. The officers are Geo. B. Cardwill, Pres.; H. E. Jewett, 1st V. P.; Geo. D. Hieb, 2d V. P.; J. O. Endris, Treas.; Chas, B. Scott, Sec ; W. A. Loughmiller, Chairman of committee on immigration, either of whom will be pleased to answer correspondence.

BUILDING AND LOAN.—The benficiary influence of building and loan associations has extended to all the states, and in many places these organizations have practically taken the place of savings banks. By these weekly or monthly payments, they encourage small savings, and by loaning to their membership, homes are easily built. This of course creates mortgages, but by the systematic payment of dues, these incumbrances are paid off in a few years, and the laboring man may become the possessor of his own home. The saloon man or demagogue, may cry that the people are being overwhelmed with mortgages, but there is no better evidence of general prosperity, than numerous well conducted building and loan associations. New Albany is particularly favored in that direction. as there are 5 thriving associations with their headquarters here, and a number of other first class companies represented by local agents.

These associations are practically co-operative savings banks, and that they have become immensely popular with the people may be gleaned from the fact that G. W. Smith, No. 48, E. Main st., treasurer for 3 of our B. & L's., handled more than half a million of dollars on that account in the year just passed. The saving of $10.000 a week, by the working people of this city, speaks volumes in itself. It tells of a prosperous city, and temperate industrious wageworkers. Philadelphia, the city that originated these societies 50 years ago, has become a city of homes, and strikes are almost unheard of there. Bring on your manufactories to keep the people employed, and then the wageworker determines to secure a home from weekly savings. Less money, will then be spent foolishly and the temperate industrious father conferring a blessing upon himself and family by small savings will eventually secure a permanent home.

The first organization of this character in New Albany, was the Floyd Co. B. & L., which was started some 20 years ago, and divided into 5 series which paid out in a little over six years. The New Albany was started some 15 years ago, and paid out in 7 years. The Citizens Savings started 4 series, and although alive is not selling stock at present.

The Home Loan was organized Jan. 1, 87, on a perpetual charter, and to accommodate its many patrons, opens a new series every 2 months, whether the former

$100,000 series is full or not. It is now working on the twenty-third. Each share of $250, costs the holder 50 cts. a week. The officers are F. M. Tribbey, Pres.; I. A. Craig, V. P.; G. B. Cardwill. Sec.; G. W. Smith, Treas.

The Workingmen's Building, was organized Mar. 17, 1890, and to accommodate small payments the shares were made $100 each, calculated to mature in 10 years upon payments of 10 cts. each week. This places the amount so small that many children invest, and are educated to small savings at an early age. Geo. E. Sackett, Pres.; W. H. McKay, V. P.; D. M. Hammond, Sec.; G. M. Smith, Treas.; E. G. Henry, Atty., for both the above.

The Peoples B. & L. was organized Jan. 89, with authorized capital of a million dollars and charter perpetual. It met with the usual favor, and has now in operation some 2,500 shares. Robt. W. Morris, Pres.; Phil. Helfrich, V. P.; Wm. R. Atkins, Treas.; and Chas. Schwartzel, for 5 years past in insurance business, is Sec., with office corner of Bank and Spring streets.

Howard Park Association was organized April, 1887, on the perpetual plan, stock to mature in 7 years. The capital, one million, is divided into 4,000 shares of $250 each, dues 50 cents per week. Levi L. Pierce, Pres.; Geo. B. Cardwill, Treas.; N. D. Morris, Sec.; E. B Stotsenburg, Att'y.

Mechanics B. & L. Association was organized Mar. 1890. Plan perpetual, 5,000 shares of $200 each. This is planned to mature in ten years on dues of 20 cts. per week. Geo. B. Cardwill, Pres.; I. A. Craig, V. P.; E. J. Hewitt, Sec.; N. D. Morris, Agt.; Herman Knirihm, Treas., E. B. Stotsenburg, Atty.

East End Building & Savings, was organized Oct. 1, 1891, authorized capital $250,000, in 1,250 shares, to be reissued as bought in by the company, making it perpetual. Wm. A. Hedden, Pres.; Hugh Nealy, Sec.; Ed. F. Trunk, Treas.

B. & L. Dept. Mutual Life & Endowment has an agency here with Marsh & Needham, and is one of the established institutions of this State. It was incorporated in Indianapolis, Feb. 17, 1882, and has matured its stock regularly in six years. On shares of $100, a monthly payment of 80 cts is made. Dr. H. J. Needham, local Sec. & Treas.

The Kentucky B. & L. was organized in June, 1891, and based upon dues at 60 cts. per month per share, will mature in 7 years. The home office is Louisville. and Frank C. Marsh, N. E. cor. Bank & Market, has been selected as Sec. & Treas. of local trade.

MERCANTILE INTERESTS.

While the manufacturing interests of a place are momentous, large and well conducted mercantile houses are important, and greatly assist in keeping at home the trade which would otherwise seek an outlet elsewhere. New Albany, although under the shadow of Louisville, is well represented in all lines of mercantile trade. Our space at present, is very limited, but we shall endeavor to make a brief mention of some representative houses in the various lines of trade.

Among the early merchants of New Albany, Paxson & Eastman, were prominent for several years from 1817. E. Baldwin commenced a year or two later, and Elias Ayres, who opened a store in 1821, continued in successful business here for many years. David Hedden, is fully mentioned under Hedden Dry Goods Co. Jesse J. Brown, a native of Baltimore, came to New Albany in 1837, and after a 3 years course at Anderson's Collegiate Institute, began clerking in the P. O. for A. S. Burnett, He was some time with David Hedden, and Shields & Lyman. In 1848 he began in the hardware store of James Brooks, becoming a partner in 47, and in 51, purchasing Mr. Brook's interest. Mr. Brown continued in the retail and jobbing hardware trade for several years, and upon the formation of the First National Bank he was selected as president, which position he held during the life of its first charter, and still continues as vice president of this well known monetary institution.

MANN & FAWCETT—Wholesale Groceries, 111, State St.

The oldest merchant now in active business here is John Mann, who was born in N. Y. May 28, 1814, came to this place in childhood, and has been in mercantile business since 1849. He commenced wholesale grocery trade in 1857, Elwood Fawcett coming into the firm in 1874, when the style became J. Mann & Co., and in 1879, upon the retirement of a third partner, the present title was adopted. Mr. Fawcett is a native of Ohio, has resided in this city for 37 years and has been in mercantile business from boyhood. The house deals exclusively in wholesale groceries occupying a complete 3 story and basement brick block, 25x120 feet, with its wares, which comprises a complete line of staple and fancy groceries. The trade of this firm is well established in a majority of Indiana towns within a radius of 130 miles from this centre, and is an important factor in New Albany's commercial trade.

P. N. CURL—General Merchandise, 202-4, W. Main.

That men of the right mettle can succeed in the mercantile trade here, has been clearly shown by numerous instances, but perhaps there is no better illustration of the self made merchant, in New Albany, than the above named gentleman. Born in Morrow Co., Ohio, Mr. Curl came to this city in 1877, and starting in the grocery trade with less than $500; he selected a location below Seventh, near the west end of Main street, where he has not only built up a very large retail trade, but is doing a jobbing business of no mean importance. Mr. Curl seems to have had a quick appreciation of the wants of his customers, and a willingness to meet every reasonable demand of business. By keeping squarely abreast of the requirements, his patrons rapidly increased and his stock of necessity grew in all directions. The large 2½ story building, a hundred feet deep, became inadequate to hold the same, and last year, he erected the fine brick and stone block adjoining, which is fitted with a cash system and modern conveniences, is 110 feet in depth, and 3 stories in heigth, and which together with the one formerly occupied, is now full on all floors. Mr. Curl carries many thousands of dollars in stock, and has one of the most complete general stores in New Albany. His wholesale grocery trade extends for a hundred miles, and his retail stock, in addition to groceries, meats and provisions, contains a complete line of dry goods, clothing, furnishings, boots, shoes and notions. That he has built up this extensive mercantile trade in 15 years, speaks not only of business tact and energy, but a good surrounding country, and substantial business city, in which to do business.

J. Zinsmeister & Bro., do an extensive wholesale trade, and G. W. McClintick conducts a jobbing and retail store. There are about 140 retail grocers.

McDonald & Co. conduct an extensive wholesale grain trade. L. Hartman and others handle flour, and we have three flour mills with aggregate capacity of 350 barrels daily.

THE F. WUNDERLICH CO.—Wholesale Liquors and Bitters.

Frederick Wunderlich, a native of Germany, has been connected with the wholesale whisky trade since 1865, commencing business alone in 1875. In 1885, the late L. Michel, son-in-law, became a partner, continuing until his death in Feb. 89. In May following the concern was incorporated as above. The company produce the "Stylus Club" Sour Mash, are manufacturers of the celebrated Aromatique Stomach Bitters, and handle at wholesale all kinds of wines and liquors. Many years in trade has brought a large business to this house, which occupies handsome rooms in the Masonic block, corner Pearl and Spring streets.

J. C. TOOPS & SON—Poultry Packers, 33, State Street.

The poultry trade of this vicinity has become a business of no mean importance, and among the best established houses in that line stands the above firm. The father and son are both Hoosiers, the senior partner having been in the poultry trade for 22 years, and for 12 years past packing an average of 350,000 pounds of dressed fowls annually, which are shipped on ice to New York. These are raised in the surrounding counties of Ind. and Ky. William, the son, is familiar with every deail. The firm handles large quantities of eggs, have met with an encouraging uccess, and have added to the commercial output of the city.

HEDDEN DRY GOODS CO.—Cor. State and Market Streets.

This firm has recently been named after one of New Albany's most venerable and espected citizens, David Hedden, who in his 90th year, still resides on Dewey street, ow having been connected with the interests of this city for nearly 72 years. He vas born at Newark, N. J., Sept. 5th, 1802, leaving there Sept. 25, 1820, with John : Charles Alling, who brought a stock of merchandise to Madison, Ind. Mr. Hedden continued down the river, landing here Nov. 1820, and shortly afterwards commenced clerking with Ebenezer Baldwin. A year or two later, he engaged with Eli-s Ayres, with whom he became a partner in 1829. Silas Day was added to this rm in 1836, the firm after Mr. Ayres demise becoming Hedden, Day & Co. For ten ears from 1846, Mr. Hedden was engaged in the milling business and has been vari-usly connected with New Albany's continued developments, still holding large real state interests.

The firm of Hedden, Phelps & Co., was organized in Oct., 1878, continuing to do n extensive trade under that style, until the incorporation of the above company, March 1st, of the present year. The capital stock was made $25,000. Wm. A. Hedlen, president of the company, has been for 30 years in mercantile trade here, and ias gained a wide reputation, as a business man, from his successful management of he Hosiery Mills. W. A. Beach, who gives constant personal charge to the store, a iative of Washington Co., Ind., has been in mercantile trade for 10 years, in con-iection with this house.

The salesroom on Market street, is 38x65 feet, and thoroughly filled with a com-plete stock of general dry goods, notions and hosiery. This opens in the rear with he State street L, 38x63 feet, three floors of which is occupied with the wares of the ompany. In this department is found an assortment of dress goods which for style, quality and prices compares favorably with the largest metropolitan stores, and it is only fancy and not necessity which requires any lady to go away from New Albany, n this line. An immense assortment of lace curtains, cloaks, etc., is also found here, vhile the Hedden Dry Goods Co. give special attention to meet the requirements of ll in hosiery and notions.

Wm. Brown & Son.—This house was started in 1867 by Wm. Brown, subse-juent to which the son was added to the firm, and the present partners are Herman 3rown and Henry A. Goetz. The above firm has secured an extensive trade in the arming community, and the retail business of the house in agricultural implements nd machinery is not exceeded by any in the Falls Cities. Fertilizers and seeds are lso important articles of trade. Occupying three floors at Nos. 77-79 State street, n immense stock is kept on hand, and among the prominent specialties in farming nachinery may be mentioned Studebaker wagons, Buckeye reapers and mowers, Su-ierior wheat drills, several standard makes of plows, corn planters, cultivators, hay presses, hay rakes, etc., in fact any machine or implement needed upon the farm. his house also commands an extensive trade in carriages and buggies and is among he solidest mercantile establishments in New Albany.

Jas. S. Peake was born in this city Jan. 9, 1834, and has stood behind the ounter for the past 40 years. In 1871 he commenced as a partner with John Baer, nd after 7 years moved to his present stand at No. 48, E. Market street. Mr. Peake :eeps a well selected, reliable and complete line of drygoods. His 40 years of trade n this city, has brought numerous customers who stand by him.

COAL INTERESTS.

Otto Hoffman has extensive coal yards, elevator, etc., at foot of Fifteenth street, nd handles upwards of a million bushels annually, requiring 25 hands and a number f teams. Mr. Hoffman is a partner in the Light, Heat & Power Co., and is among ur successful Germans.

Some 4 other firms do a like business, and as mentioned in our manufacturing in-ustries, there is no lack for cheap coal. Short space prevents further mention.

CARRIAGES, WAGONS, BLACKSMITHING, ETC.

LEWIS HANS—Carriages, cor. E. 3d & R. R.

Born in Germany, Lewis Hans has resided in New Albany from childhood, and served as engineer on a gun bo it in the late war. Returning to this city he engaged in the manufacture of carriages and other vehicles in 1865, and has ever since continued on the above corner, during which time he has turned out many fine rigs to the order of customers. The extensive carriage manufacturers have perfected labor saving machinery, until small concerns are unable to compete in prices, and many of the vehicles in Mr. Hans' sales room are from eastern manufacturers; but he is prepared to build, to the order of customers, any desirable vehicle not kept in stock.

F. W. TRIBBEY & BRO.—Carriages, Buggies, Etc.

F. M. Tribbey commenced the manufacture of carriages, etc., in this city, in 1859, and has made many hundred of vehicles. In 1890 Frances W. became a partner with his father, and Nov. last, John H., another son, took the remaining interest. The Tribbey Brothers have been raised in the business, and are expert carriage makers. They occupy three stories at 16ᵗ, Pearl street, and manufacture to the order of customers, any desirable vehicle in the most approved style of the art, keeping in stock a large assortment of carriages and buggies. Blacksmithing and wagon repair work receive prompt attention.

D. C. Axline, of Virginia, has been for 40 years in this line of trade, and also manufactures and keeps stock goods at 68, E. Third street.

There are several others who keep carriages for sale, and a number of blacksmith and wagon shops that do repair work, but no large manufactory in this line.

W. H. STEPHENS—Wood Engraver, cor. Bank & Spring.

There is no profession more exacting in its demands, or which requires more thorough training of the eye and muscle, than that of the engraver and designer. Lee H. Stephens, a native of Corydon, here from childhood, after a course in our High school, completed his studies in engraving at the Courier-Journal office, and for 7 years past has been in the business here. The success has met his most sanguine expectations, and by superior work, at reasonable prices, he is kept extremely busy, filling orders for New York and distant cities, as well as controlling the best business of the local trade. This is a special line of business, bringing money direct to our city, and we are glad to notice its success.

GREER W. DAVIS—Calcium Light Points.

The old plan of whitling out lime points has been vastly improved upon by G. W. Davis, a native of Jackson, Mo., who has resided in this city for 20 years past. He began experimenting in 1875, and by improved machinery, now turns out the most perfect point in the market. The plant is in the basement of 112, Bank street, where a complete set of lathes, gives a capacity of 14 doz. points per day. These are packed in screw top cans and shipped to the best supply houses in New York, Chicago and other metropolitan cities, for use in stereoptican and theatre scenic work.

P. M. MATHERS—Agent Bar Lock Type Writer.

The manufacturers of this successful writing machine claim for it advantages over all others in: visible writing, automatic paper feed, rapid release of carriage, permanent and perfect allignment, rapid writing, light and short depression of keys, automatic ribbon reverse, duplicate key board, almost noiseless, and the best manifold machine on the market. The agent is prepared to substantiate the above claims and illustrate other desirable features. Call on him at W. U. Tel. office.

SINGER MANF'G CO.—Cor. Bank & Spring Sts.

No other sewing machine has achieved the extent of popularity which has been accorded to the "Singer," as its more than ten million of sales will testify. Singer machines are now in use in every civilized country on the globe, and still they sell. An office was established here some 30 years ago, which for 16 years past has been in charge of J. W. Argo. The Agency covers Floyd Co., and since its establishment in New Albany, several thousands of this standard machine have been placed in the homes of this county. There are other machine agents here.

THE BUILDING INTERESTS.

GOETZ-MITCHELL—Box Anchor and Post Caps.

Any system of building which assists in preventing the spread of fire, and lessens the danger consequent upon falling walls, is an important step in architecture. Recognizing the undesirability of the old star and S anchors, which mar the beauty of buildings, and in case of fire assist in pulling down the brick wall, our townsmen, Henry A. Goetz and Mancell W. Mitchell, in 1888, patented a very important article, called the Box Anchor. This is a cast iron box of dovetail form which is built in the wall, and into which the fitted end of the joice is inserted. This is invisible from the the outside, serves every purpose of the old anchor in holding the wall together, and in case of fire as the joists burn off and fall, they simply turn themselves out of the box anchor without disturbing the wall. This was an innovation in building and it required two or three years for introduction, but has stood every reasonable test. It has been tried by the U. S. testing machine at Watertown, and found to be stronger than any other anchor. The National Association of Fire Engineers have recommended it; all insurance companies approve it, and the New England Mutuals require it in standard construction. This anchor was awarded the Scott medal by the Franklin Institute for conspicuous merit, and the proprietors have numerous testimonials, the substance of which in brief are: "The Goetz-Mitchell patents have my unqualified approval, as they are the best 1 have ever seen." More than 90 wholesale firms, from the Atlantic to the Pacific coast, have become agents and secured the right to manufacture on royalty. In connection with the box anchor, and of similar utility, is the Goetz Post Cap. In the phenominal city of Chicago these inventions have been more largely used than elsewhere, but from their approved merit they can scarcely fail of general introduction, and the proprietors Henry A. Goetz, John Goetz and Herman Brown, at 77-9, State street, may well be congratulated for the important addition to New Albany's success and manufacturing interests, which is daily growing out of the Goetz-Mitchell Box Anchor and Post Cap, that are now in use in hundreds of buildings of the best architectural construction. The Goetz Box Anchor Co. is prepared to make bids and furnish anchors and caps for buildings anywhere in the U. S. or Canada.

I. A. CRAIG—Contractor, 112, E. 9th Street.

Born in Orange Co., Ind., Isaac A. Craig has resided here for 40 years, his father, Wm. Craig, engaging in the building interest of New Albany, in 1852. In 72, I. A. Craig and Thos. Gifford commenced contracting, this partnership continuing until 1890, since when the business has been continued by Mr. Craig, who has superintended the erection of many of New Albany's fine residences. Among recent public buildings he has remodeled St. Mary's church, and erected the elegant Second Presbyterian church, corner 13th and Elm, having just completed the handsome parsonage adjoining.

JOHN NAFIUS—Contractor, 83, Market Street.

Capt. John Nafius, a native of Pa., came to New Albany in 1848, and commenced in contract work which he still continues. He has erected many of the business blocks, the Masonic Hall, old I. O. O. F. Hall, City Hall, and a full share of the residences in this place. He is this season erecting the finest school building in the city, located on Vincennes street. He employs an average of 15 to 20 mechanics.

WM. BANES—Contractor, Corner E. 9th and Market Streets.

A native of Philadelphia, Wm. Banes, has been in contract work for 50 years, commencing here with his brother, the late J. T. Banes, in 1852. In his 40 years of work in New Albany, Mr. B. has erected some of the finest residences in the city, and has added largely to the architectural beauty of the place.

CLOTHING MANUFACTURING INTERESTS.

The history of New Albany's manufacturing interests would be far short of complete, if we failed to give due notice to the houses engaged in making Jeans pants, and the tailors employed in custom clothing, together aggregating 300 to 400 persons and distributing in weekly wages many hundreds of dollars.

NEW ALBANY CLOTHING CO.—No. 38, E. Main St.

This company was incorporated Jan. 18th, 1891, with capital of $50,000, for the development of the Jeans pants trade. Operations were commenced in April, and the company occupy nearly the entire four floors of the double front brick block, at Nos. 38 and 40, East Main street. About 100 persons are employed. Some 60 sewing and buttonhole machines are in use, and with the development of trade it is contemplated to make a large addition in machinery. The present capacity is 75 dozens of pants daily, and as this house is gaining an enviable reputation for well made goods and rapidly widening its trade, extensive additions to the capacity are contemplated in the near future All the different grades of Jeans pants are turned out, in sizes to suit the demands of the trade, and as the New Albany Clothing Co. gives employment chiefly to sewing women, it opens a branch of manufacture needed by our diversified interests. The product of this concern finds a ready market, through large jobbing houses in various sections of the country.

Geo. F. Penn, president of the company is a native of Ky., residing in this city since 1866, was formerly with the Rail Mill, and for many years past has been connected with the DePauw glass works. Mr. Penn is president of the common council and has shown an active interest in New Albany's success. Wm. A. Hedden connected with the Hosiery Mills and Hedden Dry Goods Co. is vice president. Miss Ella Barnes, for several years cashier in Kraft's mercantile house, officiates as secretary and treasurer.

This company annually uses many thousand bolts of Jeans, a considerable portion of which is manufactured at the New Albany Woolen Mills, and its success adds largely to the manufacturing importance of this city.

J. M. ROBINSON & CO.—Jeans Pants Manufactory.

The advantages for cheap living and conveniences for securing help, attracted J. M. Robinson & Co., of Louisville, to locate one of their manufactories here, with the commencement of this year. The company purchased the plant formerly run by T. W. Armstrong, secured additional room, made extensive additions to the capacity and now turn out about 1,000 pairs of Jeans pants daily. The premises occupied are over 4 store rooms at the corner of Pearl and Spring streets, extending back to the alley. About 160 hands find employment, and the company contemplate erecting a large factory during the coming season. P. B. Robinson, is the New Albany manager. Such institutions tend to the rapid development of the city, and should be welcomed by every good citizen.

MERCHANT TAILORING & GENTS' FURNISHINGS.

C. C. Brown, born in New York, was reared in New Albany, and learned the tailors trade 20 years ago. Ten years since he commenced in merchant tailoring, has always endeavored to keep pace with the times, and with the first of the year, secured the light and commodious rooms at No. 40, E. Market street. A merchant tailor, in manufacturing for special customers, must use reliable goods, employ only competent workmen, and keep abreast of the times, in styles, to keep trade. Mr. Brown learned the latest system of cutting from A. D. Rude, of Cleveland, and having carefully studied the wants of his customers is prepared to meet every requirement in style, finish, and desirability of goods. Employing an average of 18 to 20 tailors, he is able to promptly turn out suits to the order of customers.

www.ingramcontent.com/pod-product-compliance
Lightning Source LLC
Chambersburg PA
CBHW031439270326
41930CB00007B/780